EXPERIENCE
HAWAIIAN ISLANDS
LIKE A FIRST
TIMER

A Guide To The Big Island, Oahu, Kauai, Maui and other Regions

John H. Leon

Copyright © by John H. Leon 2025.

All rights reserved.

Except for brief quotations used in critical reviews and other non-commercial uses permitted by copyright law, no part of this publication may be copied, distributed, or transmitted in any way without the publisher's prior written consent, including by photocopying, recording, or other electronic or mechanical methods.

The use of any trademarks or brands mentioned in this book is solely for the purpose of clarification and is not intended to imply any affiliation with the respective owners of those marks or brands.

Map of Hawaiian Islands

[Click here to View the Map of Hawaiian Islands](#)
(For e-book readers)

Scan the QR Code below with your mobile phone's Camera to View the Map of Hawaiian Islands (For Paperback Readers).

TABLE OF CONTENTS

Map of Hawaiian Islands

INTRODUCTION

   The Vibrant Culture and Heritage of Hawaii

CHAPTER 1 Practical Tips for Travelers

   Packing Essentials for Hawaii

   Health and Safety Tips for Tropical Travel

   How to Avoid Tourist Traps in Hawaii

   Currency, Banking, Tipping Etiquette and Budgeting in Hawaii

CHAPTER 2 Planning Your Trip

   Visa and Entry Requirements for Hawaii

   Essential Travel Apps and Websites for Hawaii

   Connectivity: Wi-Fi Availability, SIM Cards, and Communication

   Language and Useful Phrases in Hawaiian

CHAPTER 3 Transportation in Hawaii

   Getting There: Flights to Honolulu, Maui, Kauai, Big Island, and Other Islands

   Getting Around: Interisland Flights, Local

Shuttles, and Rental Options

Navigating Honolulu: Public Transport, Car Rentals, and Taxis

Exploring Hawaii: Tips for Island Hopping

CHAPTER 4 Accommodation in Hawaii

Luxury Stays: Five-Star Resorts and Boutique Hotels on Major Islands

Mid-Range Options: Comfortable Hotels and Condos Across Hawaii

Budget-Friendly Accommodations: Hostels and Budget Hotels Throughout the Islands

Unique Stays: Eco-Resorts, Beachside Bungalows, and Plantation Houses

CHAPTER 5 Culinary Delights Across Hawaii

Traditional and Modern Hawaiian Cuisine

Regional Specialties by Island

Best Dining Experiences: Top Restaurants and Local Eateries

Food Tours and Coffee Plantation Visits

CHAPTER 6 Shopping and Souvenirs in Hawaii

Best Shopping Districts: Honolulu, Lahaina, Kailua-Kona

Traditional Hawaiian Goods: Koa Wood, Ukuleles, and Aloha Shirts

Local Markets and Artisan Shops: Handcrafted Goods and Unique Finds

CHAPTER 7 Nightlife and Entertainment in Hawaii

Vibrant Nightlife: From Honolulu Clubs to Maui Beach Bars

Live Music and Traditional Hawaiian Hula Shows

Best Bars and Entertainment Venues Across the Islands

CHAPTER 8 Oahu: The Heart of Hawaii

Waikiki Beach, Pearl Harbor, Diamond Head

Hidden Gems: Manoa Falls, Chinatown Arts District

Hiking in the Ko'olau Range, Surfing in the North Shore

Shave Ice, Poke Bowls

Luxury Resorts, Surf Hostels

Sunset Cruises, Luau Experiences

CHAPTER 9 Maui: The Valley Isle

Upcountry Distilleries, Paia Town

Whale Watching, Snorkeling in Molokini

Farm-to-Table Restaurants, Traditional Luau

Beachfront Resorts, Secluded Villas

Beach Bars, Local Music Venues

CHAPTER 10 Kauai: The Garden Isle

Na Pali Coast, Waimea Canyon

Koke'e State Park, Hanalei Bay

Kayaking on the Wailua River, Hiking Trails

Fresh Seafood, Taro-based Dishes

Intimate Resorts, Rainforest Retreats

Quiet Bars, Cultural Festivals

CHAPTER 11 Big Island: The Island of Adventure

Volcanoes National Park, Mauna Kea Summit

Green Sand Beach, Historic Kailua Village

Lava Tours, Stargazing

Kona Coffee, Local Breweries

Lava-view Lodges, Family-friendly Condos

Local Brewpubs, Evening Luaus

CHAPTER 12 Waikiki: Hawaii's Premier Beachfront

Waikiki Beach, Diamond Head, Royal Hawaiian Center

Kuhio Beach Park, Ala Wai Golf Course

Surfing at Waikiki Beach, hiking Diamond Head

Luau feasts, seafood along the beach

Beach bars, hula shows

CHAPTER 13 Honolulu: The Vibrant Capital

Iolani Palace, USS Arizona Memorial, Aloha Tower

Foster Botanical Garden, Shangri La Museum

Snorkeling at Hanauma Bay, biking at Kapiolani Park

Pacific Rim cuisine, local food trucks

Downtown hotels, charming guesthouses

Jazz clubs, cultural performances

CHAPTER 14 Lesser-Known Islands: Lanai and Molokai

Shipwreck Beach, Kalaupapa National Historical Park

Lanai Cat Sanctuary, Molokai's Ancient Fishponds

Off-Road Tours, Quiet Beaches

Unique Island Cuisine, Local Eateries

Exclusive Resorts, Rustic Lodges

Low-key Evenings, Cultural Talks

CHAPTER 15 Outdoor Adventures in Hawaii

Hiking and Trekking: Exploring Tropical Trails and Coastal Walks

Beaches and Water Sports: Surfing, Diving, and Sailing in Hawaiian Waters

Adventure Sports: Paragliding, Zip-lining

CHAPTER 16 Every Type of Traveler

Solo Travelers: Safe Destinations and Activities

Couples: Romantic Retreats and Private Beaches

Families: Kid-Friendly Attractions and Resorts

Groups: Activities and Large Group Accommodations

Senior Travelers: Accessible Tours and Leisure Activities

Guided Tours vs. Self-Guided Explorations

CHAPTER 17 Sample Itineraries for Hawaii

7-Day Highlights Tour of Major Islands

10-Day Deep Dive into Hawaiian Culture and Nature

Luxury 14-Day Tour: Exploring Hawaii's Natural Beauty and Exclusive Resorts

Off-the-Beaten-Path Adventures: Discovering Hidden Gems of Hawaii

Departure Checklist and Customs Regulations

CHAPTER 18 Respecting Hawaiian Culture

Understanding and Honoring Local Traditions and Etiquette

Cultural Heritage Sites: Temples, Heiaus, and Historic Villages

Sustainable Tourism: How to Visit Hawaii Responsibly

CONCLUSION

INTRODUCTION

Hawaii is a place like no other. With its sparkling blue waters, lush green landscapes, and unique culture, it draws people from all over the world. Whether you are planning a short vacation or a long stay, Hawaii offers experiences that cater to every type of traveler. The islands are not just a beautiful vacation spot; they are a world of rich traditions, exciting outdoor adventures, and unforgettable memories.

This guide is your key to unlocking everything Hawaii has to offer. Inside these pages, you will find the most up-to-date and useful information on how to plan a trip to Hawaii. From tips on what to pack to how to explore each island, this book is designed to make your trip easier, more enjoyable, and most importantly, unforgettable.

You will learn about the best times to visit each island, the hidden gems that many tourists overlook, and the must-see attractions that make Hawaii famous. Whether it's the stunning beaches of Oahu, the breathtaking views on Maui, or the volcanic wonders of the Big Island, each island has its own special charm and story to tell.

The guide will also help you navigate Hawaii's transportation options, from flights between islands to the best local ways of getting around. It will introduce you to the unique food of Hawaii, from traditional dishes to modern takes on island flavors. For those who enjoy shopping, you will discover the best spots to find Hawaiian-made goods and souvenirs, as well as where to enjoy the local nightlife and entertainment.

Beyond the basics of travel, this guide goes deeper into understanding Hawaiian culture. It explains how to respect the local traditions and customs, ensuring that your visit is both enjoyable and respectful to the islanders who call Hawaii home. Whether you are here for the natural beauty, the culture, or the adventure, this book will help you experience Hawaii in the best way possible.

Packed with practical advice, insider tips, and carefully selected recommendations, this guide will be your companion every step of the way. As you read through these pages, you will find yourself dreaming about the experiences waiting for you in Hawaii. And once you step foot on the islands, you will feel confident and excited, knowing you have the best information at your fingertips.

By the time you finish this book, you will not only be prepared for your trip—you will be eager to start your adventure. With this guide in hand, Hawaii will feel less like a faraway dream and more like your next unforgettable journey.

The Vibrant Culture and Heritage of Hawaii

Exploring the vibrant culture and heritage of Hawaii has been one of the most enriching experiences of my life. As I journeyed through the islands, I realized that Hawaii is much more than its pristine beaches and stunning landscapes. It's a place where every breeze and wave seems to tell a story, and every tradition invites you to step a little deeper into its rich history.

Hawaii's culture is a colorful tapestry woven from the many different peoples who have made these islands their home. From the original Polynesian navigators who first settled here over a thousand years ago, to the various immigrants who arrived during the plantation era, each group has contributed to the cultural kaleidoscope of Hawaii. The result is a community deeply rooted in a heritage of aloha—a concept that extends beyond greeting to a genuine compassion for others.

Dance and music are pillars of Hawaiian culture, with the hula being perhaps the most iconic. My first encounter with hula was at a local festival on Oahu. The dancers, adorned in skirts of ti leaves and garlands of flowers, moved with a grace that seemed to capture the very soul of the islands. The chants and songs accompanying the dance told stories of love, heroism, and the deep connections the Hawaiian people have with the land.

Another aspect of Hawaiian culture that fascinated me is their language. Hawaiian, with its melodious flow and fewer than a dozen consonants, was once banned in schools in a bid to westernize the islands. However, the language has seen a revival and is taught in schools and universities as a point of pride and a means of preserving heritage. Learning a few phrases, like "Mahalo" (thank you) and "Aloha" (hello, goodbye, love), helped me connect more deeply with the locals.

Feasts, or luaus, are another cultural hallmark where the community and visitors alike can indulge in traditional foods like poi (a starchy paste made from taro), kalua pig (cooked in an earth oven), and poke (seasoned raw fish). Attending a luau taught me about the Hawaiian way of celebrating life's milestones—births, victories, and even a visitor's first trip to the islands—with food, song, and stories.

Craftsmanship in Hawaii also tells a story of cultural heritage, from the intricate weaving of lauhala hats to the crafting of koa wood into beautiful furniture and ukuleles. I spent a fascinating afternoon with a local artisan who shared how each piece of koa wood is as unique as the island itself, with deep grains and hues that echo the diverse landscapes of Hawaii.

The spirit of 'ohana (family) permeates every aspect of Hawaiian life. This concept extends beyond blood relations to encompass friends, neighbors, and visitors. It's about treating everyone with respect and kindness. During my stay, I was embraced as part of this 'ohana, which made my journey even more special.

Through my travels across Hawaii, I've learned that to truly experience the islands, one must dive into its cultural depths. It's not just about seeing the sights; it's about immersing oneself in the stories, traditions, and community life. This is what I aim to share with you through this guide. So, as you turn these pages and make your way to these enchanting islands, remember that you're not just a visitor—you're part of a continuing story, and every step teaches you more about the vibrant culture and heritage of Hawaii.

CHAPTER 1

Practical Tips for Travelers

Packing Essentials for Hawaii

When I first set foot on Hawaii's shores, I quickly learned that packing isn't as simple as just throwing in a swimsuit and sunscreen. The islands, with their tropical climate, varying landscapes, and outdoor-focused lifestyle, require a thoughtful approach to what you bring. Whether you're exploring rainforests, hiking volcanic craters, or lounging on the beach, packing the right essentials can make or break your trip.

One thing I didn't realize until I got there is how quickly the weather can shift. You might wake up to a sunny morning in Waikiki, but by afternoon, you could be caught in a tropical shower. This is why lightweight, breathable clothing is a must. I recommend packing a mix of shorts, tank tops, and light long sleeves. These are perfect for the warm days but will also give you some coverage if you find yourself in the sun for long stretches. You'll also want to make sure you have something for those cooler evenings—especially if you're heading up to higher elevations like Haleakalā National Park on Maui or the volcanoes on the Big Island. A light jacket or sweater will do just fine for those chilly moments after sunset.

Footwear is another area where I learned the importance of being practical. Sure, flip-flops are a staple in Hawaii, and you'll definitely want a pair for the beach, but if you plan to do any hiking (and trust me, you'll want to), make sure you pack a sturdy pair of sneakers or trail shoes. I made the mistake of wearing sandals on a hike along the Na Pali Coast in Kauai and ended up with sore feet by the end of the day. A good pair of shoes will make a world of difference, especially if you're venturing into rugged terrain or trying to tackle a steep climb to a waterfall. Another packing must-have is sun protection. I quickly learned that the sun in Hawaii is intense, even on cloudy days. So, sunscreen is non-negotiable. I opted for reef-safe sunscreen because it protects both my skin and the delicate marine life. I also recommend packing a wide-brimmed hat and sunglasses with UV protection—these will not only keep you comfortable but also protect your eyes from the strong Hawaiian rays. On the same note, I found that a reusable water bottle was essential. The islands' heat can quickly leave you dehydrated, and keeping a water bottle with you at all times is a simple yet effective way to stay hydrated while exploring.

If you're planning on spending time in the ocean, which you absolutely should, don't forget swimwear and, if you're into snorkeling, a snorkel mask. Hawaii's waters are home to some of the most incredible marine life, and having your own gear can save you time and money. I also learned that water shoes are a good idea, especially if you plan on visiting some of the more rugged beaches or rocky shorelines. The beaches are beautiful, but the volcanic rocks can sometimes make it tricky to walk comfortably without the right footwear.

For the tech-savvy traveler, don't forget your chargers, portable power bank, and any other gadgets you might need to capture all the amazing moments. However, I'll say this: try not to overdo it with electronics. I found that the beauty of Hawaii is in its nature, and sometimes it's nice to disconnect. That said, a good camera (or even your smartphone) will be essential for capturing the iconic landscapes, from the dramatic cliffs of Kauai to the sunset views of Maui's beaches.

Finally, something I wasn't prepared for but quickly learned to appreciate is packing a light rain jacket. In places like Kauai, you'll find that it rains often and unexpectedly. Having a compact, lightweight rain jacket tucked away in your bag means you won't be caught off guard when the skies open up.

Packing for Hawaii requires a little more forethought than simply preparing for a beach vacation. But once you have these basics covered, you'll be set for nearly anything the islands can throw at you. From tropical rainstorms to sun-drenched hikes, having the right gear on hand will help you make the most of your time in paradise. After all, Hawaii is an adventure waiting to happen, and with the right packing list, you can be ready for all of it.

Health and Safety Tips for Tropical Travel

When I first arrived in Hawaii, I was immediately taken in by the islands' beauty and vibrant energy, but I quickly realized that there are some unique health and safety considerations when traveling to a tropical destination like this one. After all, Hawaii's climate, landscape, and environment can present challenges that travelers might not be used to back home. So, before I packed my bags, I made sure to brush up on a few health tips and safety precautions to ensure that my trip was as enjoyable and smooth as possible.

One of the first things I learned is that the sun in Hawaii is no joke. It's stronger than what you might be used to, especially if you're coming from a cooler climate. The last thing you want on your dream vacation is a painful sunburn, so applying sunscreen regularly is essential. I made sure to use reef-safe sunscreen, not just because it protects the environment but also because it's great for your skin. You'll want to apply it every two hours, or more often if you're swimming or sweating. I learned that the hard way when I forgot to reapply after snorkeling and ended up with a sunburn I'd rather forget. Don't make the same mistake—protect yourself before you even feel the burn.

Speaking of water, staying hydrated is crucial when you're in a tropical place like Hawaii. The weather can be warm and humid, and if you're out exploring or hiking, you'll lose water more quickly than you realize. I found that carrying a reusable water bottle with me at all times was one of the best things I could do. Not only does it keep you hydrated, but it also helps reduce plastic waste, which is something the locals really appreciate. Plus, it's easy to find water refill stations around the islands, so you don't have to keep buying bottled water.

Hiking and outdoor activities are some of the best ways to experience Hawaii, but I quickly learned that the trails, while stunning, can also be challenging and even risky. One thing that caught me off guard was the muddy conditions on some of the trails, particularly in places like Kauai, where rain is frequent. The mud can get slippery, and if you're not careful, you could easily slip. So, I recommend packing sturdy shoes with good tread—trust me, this will save you from taking a tumble. I also noticed that many trails on the islands are quite exposed to the sun, so I made sure to wear a hat and long sleeves to protect myself from the sun while hiking.

Another health consideration is the potential for mosquito bites, especially in the more tropical areas. While Hawaii isn't known for dangerous diseases carried by mosquitoes, I still made sure to pack insect repellent and wear it when I was venturing into the forests or wetlands. Nothing ruins a peaceful evening like a dozen itchy bites, so taking preventive measures is a good idea, particularly if you plan to do any hiking or visit areas near water.

It's also important to be aware of the ocean's power. While the beaches are absolutely inviting, the ocean can be tricky. Whether you're swimming, surfing, or snorkeling, always pay attention to warning signs, surf conditions, and lifeguards. Hawaii has some of the most powerful waves in the world, especially on the North Shore of Oahu and during the winter months. I had to learn the hard way that not all beaches are suitable for beginners, and some spots have strong rip currents that can pull you out to sea. Always swim at beaches with lifeguards, and make sure you're comfortable with the water conditions before heading out. If you're not an experienced swimmer, consider staying in shallow areas or trying out snorkeling from a boat or a calm bay where the water is gentler.

Another tip I wish I'd known before my first trip is the importance of being mindful of the wildlife. While most animals in Hawaii aren't dangerous, there are a few things to watch out for. For example, certain sea creatures like jellyfish can be found in the waters, and their stings can be painful. While I was lucky enough to avoid one during my trip, I made sure to heed all local warnings and pay attention to the advice given by locals and signs on the beaches.

It's also important to take care when dealing with Hawaii's natural beauty. While it's tempting to get as close as possible to lava flows, waterfalls, and cliffs for that perfect Instagram shot, be aware that these areas can be dangerous. On my hike to a secluded waterfall, I was reminded that the path can be rugged and sometimes unpredictable. Stick to marked trails and don't take unnecessary risks. I also recommend carrying a first-aid kit with some basics—band-aids, antiseptic wipes, and any medications you might need—just in case something goes wrong.

Finally, it's always a good idea to get travel insurance, particularly when traveling to a place like Hawaii where medical care can be expensive. It's better to be safe than sorry, and knowing that you're covered for any unexpected emergencies can give you peace of mind. After all, the last thing you want to worry about when you're in paradise is whether you'll be able to afford a doctor's visit if you twist your ankle on a hike or catch a cold.

By taking these health and safety tips to heart, I found that I was able to fully enjoy everything Hawaii had to offer, from the beaches to the trails, without any major hiccups. It's all about being prepared, staying aware, and respecting the natural environment around you.

How to Avoid Tourist Traps in Hawaii

When I first visited Hawaii, I was filled with excitement and wonder at the beauty of the islands, but it didn't take long to realize that some of the most popular tourist spots weren't all they were cracked up to be. The natural beauty of the islands is unmatched, but there are also plenty of tourist traps that can quickly sap your vacation experience, not to mention your wallet. Over time, I learned how to avoid these common pitfalls, and now, I want to share some of the best tips I've picked up along the way.

One of the first things I noticed was that some of the so-called "must-see" attractions in Hawaii can be overcrowded, overpriced, and sometimes, not all that exciting once you get there. The famous spots like Waikiki Beach and the Pearl Harbor Memorial are beautiful and significant, but they can also feel like a circus, especially if you're looking for a more authentic experience. It's not that these places should be avoided entirely, but if you want to escape the crowds, you'll need to plan wisely.

For example, when I first ventured to Waikiki Beach, I was thrilled by the thought of lounging on such an iconic spot. However, once I arrived, I quickly realized that the area was packed with tourists, overpriced restaurants, and beach vendors trying to sell everything from sunglasses to parasailing rides. It was far from the peaceful, relaxing beach experience I had imagined. What I ended up doing was leaving Waikiki for a day and exploring the quieter beaches on the island, like Ala Moana Beach Park or Kailua Beach. These spots were just as stunning, but with far fewer tourists and a much more laid-back vibe. The lesson I took away from this was that sometimes, the best experiences come from stepping away from the well-known tourist areas.

Another tourist trap I fell into early on was the abundance of "guided tours" that promise to show you everything, but often only take you to the same spots everyone else is visiting. Take the famous Hana Highway on Maui, for instance. While this scenic route is undoubtedly beautiful, it can be extremely congested with tour buses, especially during peak times. Many tour operators rush you through the main stops without allowing you to really enjoy or appreciate the beauty of each location. I chose to rent a car and drive the Hana Highway myself. The difference was night and day. I had the freedom to pull over when I wanted, take my time at the hidden gems along the way, and even stop for a local picnic at a lesser-known beach. The key takeaway here is that while guided tours can be helpful, they're not always the best way to experience the islands. Renting a car and exploring at your own pace often leads to far more rewarding experiences.

In the world of Hawaiian souvenirs, it's easy to be lured into the flashy tourist shops that promise unique gifts, but a lot of what you'll find in these stores is mass-produced and overpriced. I made the mistake of buying a few "authentic" trinkets from a well-known store in Waikiki, only to realize later that they were made overseas and sold for way more than they were worth. The local artisans and smaller shops, however, offer much better quality, and you're actually supporting the community. On my later trips, I sought out local markets and artisan shops, particularly in places like Lahaina or the North Shore of Oahu, where I found beautiful handmade jewelry, clothing, and wooden crafts that truly captured the spirit of the islands. The moral here is that when it comes to souvenirs, seek out local artisans and avoid the big-box tourist shops.

Food in Hawaii can also be a tricky subject. There are plenty of "tourist traps" disguised as restaurants that promise you a taste of local cuisine but often end up serving bland, overpriced meals. I fell into this trap during my first trip, choosing a beachfront restaurant because it looked picturesque, only to pay a premium for a dish that was nothing special. What I found to be much more satisfying were the local food trucks and small mom-and-pop restaurants scattered throughout the islands. These places offer real Hawaiian flavors at a fraction of the price. One of my favorite spots was a food truck near Kailua Beach that served poke bowls, fresh fish tacos, and other delicious island favorites. Not only was the food incredible, but I also got a true taste of Hawaiian culture in a more authentic and less commercialized setting.

One more thing I discovered is that the Hawaiian islands are full of natural wonders that you can easily overlook if you're caught up in the main tourist spots. I found that the best way to avoid tourist traps was to do a little research ahead of time, chat with locals, and explore some lesser-known areas. One of my favorite hidden gems was the Makapu'u Tide Pools on Oahu. It's a bit off the beaten path, but once I got there, I was rewarded with crystal-clear waters, unique volcanic rock formations, and a peaceful atmosphere away from the crowds. Another spot worth mentioning is the Pololu Valley Lookout on the Big Island. It's not as well-known as the more famous volcanoes, but it offers some of the most breathtaking views you'll find anywhere on the islands.

I also found that, when in doubt, talking to locals can help you avoid common tourist traps. I learned this when I asked a surf instructor on Oahu about hidden beaches and lesser-known spots. His advice led me to quiet places like Sandy Beach and Makena Beach, which I never would have discovered on my own. Locals know the islands like no one else, and they're often happy to share tips on where to go for the most authentic, beautiful, and less commercialized experiences.

In the end, avoiding tourist traps in Hawaii isn't about completely avoiding the famous spots—it's about knowing when to skip the crowds and look for the gems that lie just off the beaten path. With a little effort and a bit of local knowledge, you can discover the true heart of the islands, creating memories that feel authentic and unique.

Currency, Banking, Tipping Etiquette and Budgeting in Hawaii

When I first visited Hawaii, one of the things that threw me off a bit was getting used to the local currency, banking practices, and tipping customs. It wasn't as straightforward as I had imagined, and in a place as unique as Hawaii, there are a few things that can make your spending experience feel a little different from what you might expect in other parts of the U.S. So, if you're planning a trip, it helps to understand how money works in Hawaii—whether it's budgeting for your trip, knowing where to exchange currency, or figuring out how to tip.

Let's start with the basics: Hawaii uses the U.S. dollar (USD), so if you're coming from abroad, you won't need to worry about exchanging your money into a different currency. That's one less thing to deal with. But if you're like me and are visiting from a place where the exchange rate can get tricky, you'll want to avoid exchanging money at airports or tourist areas, where you'll get unfavorable rates and often have to pay hefty fees.

Instead, I found that withdrawing cash from an ATM once I got to Hawaii was one of the easiest and most cost-effective ways to get local currency. Plus, ATMs are easy to find, and most accept international cards without much hassle, though you should always check with your bank to ensure your card works there and inquire about fees.

Once I had my cash in hand, I quickly realized that credit and debit cards are widely accepted everywhere in Hawaii—restaurants, hotels, even food trucks. So, I didn't really need to carry around huge amounts of cash unless I was headed to more remote areas or doing things like buying goods at farmers' markets or small local shops that might not have card readers. However, I also made a habit of carrying some cash on me for small purchases, like tips or parking fees. The general advice is to always have a little cash, just in case, especially when you're out on the more rural islands like Kauai or the Big Island, where cash-only businesses are more common.

Banking in Hawaii is pretty similar to the rest of the U.S., but there are a couple of things to note. First, Hawaii is a bit isolated from the mainland, so if you plan to withdraw cash, make sure you have access to ATMs that don't charge foreign transaction fees. If you need to visit a bank for any reason, there are several local branches of major U.S. banks like Bank of Hawaii, First Hawaiian Bank, and Central Pacific Bank scattered throughout the islands. While the major tourist areas tend to have plenty of options, if you're heading off the beaten path, like to the smaller islands or less populated areas, it's best to plan ahead.

Next up is tipping etiquette, something I quickly had to get the hang of when I first arrived. Tipping in Hawaii follows many of the same practices you'll find across the mainland U.S., but there are some nuances to keep in mind. For instance, at sit-down restaurants, I typically tipped 15-20% of the bill, depending on the service. What surprised me was that at many of the smaller, local eateries or casual dining spots, there wasn't always a tip jar or an obvious expectation, but a tip is still appreciated. I often left a few dollars when the service was good, and it was clear that the locals were grateful for it.

For activities like tours, excursions, or even boat rides, it's common to tip tour guides and drivers. On one of my whale-watching trips, I tipped the guide $10 per person, and he seemed genuinely appreciative. It was a nice touch, especially because it made me feel like I was supporting local businesses and making the guide's day a little better. Taxi drivers, valet attendants, and hotel bellhops also expect tips. For taxi drivers, I generally gave them a tip of 10-15%, and I would tip hotel staff $1-2 per bag when they helped me with luggage.

Another part of budgeting I learned quickly was how easy it is for costs to add up when you're in Hawaii. Everything from food to activities tends to be a little pricier than what you might be used to back home, and I definitely noticed that. Dining out in Hawaii, especially in touristy areas like Waikiki, can easily cost you $30-50 per person, even at casual restaurants. I quickly learned to keep an eye out for local favorites that offered delicious food at more affordable prices. Food trucks and small family-owned places often have meals that are just as good, if not better, than the tourist spots—plus, they tend to cost much less. I remember grabbing an amazing plate of loco moco (a local dish with rice, a burger patty, gravy, and a fried egg) from a small food truck near Kailua Beach for just $10. It was filling, tasty, and way cheaper than the overpriced plates I'd been seeing at some of the restaurants along the coast.

As for activities, they can be a huge part of your budget, especially if you're planning on doing tours or renting equipment. Some activities, like hiking or visiting national parks, don't cost anything at all, but others—like helicopter tours, boat rentals, or scuba diving lessons—can be pretty pricey. One thing I did that saved me some money was pre-booking certain tours online. By researching in advance and booking a few days ahead of time, I was able to take advantage of discounts that weren't offered when I walked up on the day of the activity. Another tip is to look for package deals, where you can bundle several activities together for a lower price. It worked out really well for me on one of my snorkeling trips, where I got a great deal by booking a combo package that included both snorkeling and a visit to a local marine sanctuary.

I also made sure to set a daily spending limit for myself, which helped me avoid going overboard. Hawaii is beautiful, and there's always something tempting to spend your money on, whether it's a fancy dinner, a new piece of local artwork, or a helicopter ride over a volcano. But by sticking to a budget, I was able to enjoy all of those experiences without the guilt of overspending.

Overall, budgeting in Hawaii isn't that much different from other destinations, but it does require some thoughtful planning. By keeping an eye on currency exchange, banking, and tipping norms, I felt much more at ease navigating the financial side of things. And with a little planning and research, you'll be able to enjoy everything the islands have to offer while keeping your spending in check.

CHAPTER 2

Planning Your Trip

Visa and Entry Requirements for Hawaii

When I first started planning my trip to Hawaii, one of the first things I had to figure out was the visa and entry requirements. Even though Hawaii is a U.S. state, it's important to remember that not everyone has the same requirements when traveling there. If you're a U.S. citizen, you're in the clear—no visa needed. But for international travelers, there are a few steps to consider.

If you're coming from outside the United States, you'll need to make sure that you meet the necessary visa or entry requirements before you board your flight. I learned quickly that it's not enough to just have a passport—depending on your nationality, you might need more. For travelers from countries that are part of the Visa

Waiver Program (VWP), entering Hawaii is relatively simple. The VWP allows citizens from certain countries to travel to the U.S. (including Hawaii) for tourism purposes without a visa, as long as their stay is 90 days or less. However, you will still need to apply for an ESTA (Electronic System for Travel Authorization) before your trip. The ESTA application is easy to fill out online and typically gets approved within a few minutes, though I recommend doing it at least 72 hours before your departure to be safe.

Now, if you're not from one of those countries or you're planning to stay longer than 90 days, you'll need to apply for a tourist visa. The most common type for visitors to Hawaii is the B-2 Visitor Visa. This visa allows you to travel for leisure or tourism purposes. The process involves filling out an application form, scheduling an interview at your nearest U.S. embassy or consulate, and providing various documents, such as proof of financial stability to show you can support yourself during your trip, a return ticket to your home country, and sometimes a plan of your intended itinerary.

Once your visa is approved, entering Hawaii isn't much different than entering the U.S. mainland. You'll need to go through customs and immigration upon arrival. Be ready to present your passport, a completed customs declaration form, and any additional documents you were asked to bring. While the process might seem intimidating at first, I found that most officials are friendly and understanding. Just make sure all your paperwork is in order, and you'll breeze through it.

One thing I didn't realize before my trip was the importance of checking passport validity. Most countries require that your passport be valid for at least six months after your intended departure date from the U.S. I had nearly overlooked this detail when I was booking my flight, but I'm glad I double-checked. If your passport is set to expire too soon, it's worth renewing it before your trip.

Also, remember that U.S. immigration laws apply to Hawaii just like any other state. This means that if you've had any issues with U.S. immigration in the past, such as overstaying a visa or being deported, it could affect your ability to enter Hawaii, even though it's a domestic destination. So, it's always best to make sure your travel history is in good standing before planning a trip.

Lastly, I found that some travelers often forget to check if they need any vaccinations before visiting. While Hawaii doesn't have any mandatory vaccinations, it's always wise to double-check with your doctor or travel clinic to make sure you're up to date on any necessary immunizations for traveling in general, especially if you're coming from a region with higher health risks.

Best Time to Visit Oahu, Maui, Kauai, Big Island, and Other Islands

When I was planning my trip to Hawaii, one of the first questions I had was when exactly should I go? After all, timing can make or break a vacation, especially when you're visiting a place as diverse as the Hawaiian Islands. There are several factors to think about—weather, crowds, activities, and even the specific island you're heading to. Each island has its own vibe, and the best time to visit can vary depending on what kind of experience you're looking for.

For starters, Hawaii has pretty great weather year-round, which is one of the reasons why it's a favorite destination for so many people. The islands experience a tropical climate, with two main seasons: summer and winter. Summer, from about June to September, is warm and sunny, while winter, from December to March, is a bit cooler and wetter, especially on the northern parts of the islands. For most travelers, the summer months offer ideal beach weather, with temperatures ranging from the low 70s to mid-80s (°F), which is perfect for water sports, lounging, or hiking in the mountains.

However, the weather isn't the only factor that makes timing important—it's also about avoiding the crowds. Hawaii, especially popular islands like Oahu, Maui, and Kauai, can get packed with tourists, particularly during the peak months of December through March and again in the summer. This is when the islands see an influx of visitors, drawn by holidays, school vacations, and perfect beach weather. If you're someone who prefers a more laid-back experience, I highly recommend planning your trip during the shoulder seasons. These are typically the months just before or after the busy periods—late spring (April to June) and fall (September to November). During these months, the islands are still warm, but there are fewer tourists, and you can often find better deals on accommodations and activities.

Now, let's dive into each island specifically. If you're planning to visit Oahu, you'll find that it's one of the busiest islands, especially in Honolulu and Waikiki. For those looking to avoid the crowds, I suggest going during the off-season, from April to early June, or mid-September to November. The weather is still excellent, but you won't have to fight for space on the beach or reservations at restaurants. Plus, Oahu is a great place to visit any time of year because of its diverse activities, from hiking Diamond Head to surfing on the North Shore. I found that winter months can bring bigger waves to the North Shore, which makes it a prime time for surfing, but for someone who just wants to relax on the beach, it might not be ideal.

Maui, known for its stunning beaches and luxury resorts, is perfect for a getaway at any time of year, but it shines most in the spring and fall. These months tend to have the best combination of warm weather and fewer tourists. The Road to

Hana and Haleakala National Park are breathtaking during these months, as the scenery seems even more vibrant and the trails less crowded. I've visited Maui in both the summer and the off-peak months, and I can personally say that Maui is especially peaceful in the spring. The beaches are quieter, and it's easier to find a secluded spot for a sunset walk.

Kauai, the Garden Isle, is a dream for nature lovers. Its lush landscapes and waterfalls are best enjoyed when it's not pouring rain, which is why visiting in the late spring or early fall is ideal. I've been to Kauai during the rainy season, and while it was still beautiful, some of the hiking trails and beaches can get muddy, making it a bit trickier to explore. The months from April to June and September to November are much drier and more pleasant for outdoor activities like hiking, zip-lining, and kayaking along the Na Pali Coast.

Big Island is unique in that it offers the most variety in landscapes, from beaches to volcanoes. What I've found is that Big Island is pretty consistent weather-wise, but it can vary depending on where you are. The western side of the island, where Kailua-Kona is, is typically dry and sunny year-round, while the eastern side, where Hilo is located, is much wetter. So, when planning your trip, it's important to keep in mind what kind of activities you want. I personally recommend visiting in the late spring or fall to avoid both the heat and the crowds. It's also the best time to visit Volcanoes National Park if you want to avoid the rainy weather that can sometimes affect your experience there.

For those considering the lesser-known islands like Lanai or Molokai, I've found that they are best visited during the off-peak months. These islands tend to be less crowded and much more laid-back, so going in the spring or fall means you'll have the peace and quiet to explore these hidden gems without the rush of tourists. The weather is great year-round, but the more relaxed vibe during the off-peak seasons makes these islands feel even more special.

All in all, the best time to visit Hawaii really depends on your preferences. If you're looking for the best weather and don't mind sharing the islands with more tourists, then summer and winter are ideal. However, if you prefer fewer crowds and better deals, I'd suggest going in the shoulder seasons of spring and fall. I've been to Hawaii at various times of the year, and I can confidently say that no matter when you visit, the beauty of the islands will always make it worth the trip. It's all about what kind of experience you want to have!

Essential Travel Apps and Websites for Hawaii

When I first visited Hawaii, I quickly realized that having the right travel apps and websites on hand could really make a difference in how smoothly the trip went. With so much to see, do, and experience across the islands, it's easy to get overwhelmed or lost if you don't have the right tools. Whether it's navigating winding roads, finding local hotspots, or keeping up with changing weather patterns, having a reliable set of resources can turn a good vacation into a great one.

One of the first apps I downloaded was Google Maps. It's probably the most well-known and reliable app for navigation, but in Hawaii, where some roads can be narrow and remote, I found it to be indispensable. What I loved about it most was its ability to provide real-time traffic updates and alternate routes, especially when I was trying to avoid the more tourist-heavy areas or explore less-visited spots. It also helped me find hidden gems—beaches, parks, and even local eateries—that weren't always in the guidebooks. Google Maps works offline, which is great if you're headed to more remote areas with spotty service. But I do recommend downloading the offline maps for specific islands, just in case you find yourself somewhere without signal.

Alongside Google Maps, another essential for me was Hawaii's official tourism website, GoHawaii.com. This site is a one-stop-shop for pretty much everything you need to know about the islands. Whether you're looking for specific events happening while you're there, up-to-date information on local attractions, or even booking tours, this site offers a lot. I used it to find information on festivals, hikes, and even lesser-known beaches. The website also provides detailed maps and suggestions for itineraries, so it's easy to customize your trip based on the type of experience you're hoping to have.

For booking accommodations, Airbnb and Booking.com were my go-to apps. These are both great for finding places to stay across the islands, from private rentals to larger resorts. One thing I especially liked was how both apps allow you to filter by location, price range, and amenities—making it easy to find a place that fits your travel style, whether you're looking for a luxury resort on Maui or a cozy, budget-friendly bungalow on Kauai. I've used Airbnb in the past to book unique stays like treehouses and beach cottages, which gave me a more authentic and intimate experience with the local environment.

Once I settled on where I was staying, I realized I needed a reliable app for restaurants and food recommendations. Yelp and TripAdvisor both became indispensable for finding the best local eats. I used Yelp to check out reviews, browse menus, and see pictures from fellow travelers. Since Hawaii offers such diverse dining options—from traditional Hawaiian dishes to fusion cuisine—Yelp helped me make informed choices about where to eat. I also loved that it showed me the most popular dishes at each restaurant, so I always knew what to try first. TripAdvisor was also useful when I wanted to get an overview of the area's top restaurants and attractions, especially since it offers both user reviews and expert insights.

When it came to planning outdoor adventures, I found AllTrails to be incredibly useful for hikes and outdoor activities. Hawaii is a hiker's paradise, and AllTrails made it easy to find detailed trail maps, read reviews from fellow hikers, and get difficulty ratings for each trail. From short beach walks on Oahu to more challenging hikes up volcanoes on the Big Island, AllTrails gave me the confidence to venture out and explore. I also made sure to download the trail maps to my phone ahead of time, just in case there was limited cell service in more remote areas.

For exploring local culture, I also leaned on Hawaiian Airlines' app. Even though I wasn't flying with them during my trip, I found their app useful for tracking weather patterns, checking for last-minute flight deals if I wanted to hop between islands, and getting up-to-date information on special events and activities across the islands. It's also a good resource for flight-related updates and making last-minute changes to plans, which can happen when you're traveling in paradise.

Weather can be unpredictable in Hawaii, and knowing when a storm is coming or when the sun is out can make a big difference in your plans. The Weather Channel app was my constant companion, especially for checking rain forecasts on the islands. It was also super helpful when I was trying to figure out the best time to hit the beach or go on a boat tour, as I could monitor weather patterns in real-time. Another app I liked for weather-related details was Hawaiian Water Safety, which gave me updates on ocean conditions, such as surf heights and warnings for swimming. This became especially important when I visited more secluded beaches where conditions could change rapidly.

Finally, I found it useful to have Hawaiian Islands' official transportation apps—especially for things like renting cars or taking public transit. If you're planning to rent a car, apps like Turo (the "Airbnb for cars") or the standard Enterprise and Hertz apps help you compare prices, book vehicles, and find rental locations, often saving time and hassle. If you want to skip the car rental process altogether, apps like Uber and Lyft are widely available across the islands. On the Big Island, I also used Island Hopper for inter-island flights, which offered great deals on quick trips to explore different islands without a long flight.

These apps and websites were my constant companions throughout my trip to Hawaii, and I couldn't imagine traveling without them. They made everything—from navigating the islands to finding great places to eat—so much easier and more enjoyable. With the right apps in your pocket, you'll have everything you need to make your Hawaiian vacation smooth, fun, and full of unforgettable experiences.

Connectivity: Wi-Fi Availability, SIM Cards, and Communication

When I first landed in Hawaii, one of the things I was most curious about was staying connected while I was exploring the islands. Being in a remote part of the world, I was unsure about how easy it would be to get reliable Wi-Fi or cellular service. As it turns out, staying connected in Hawaii is fairly straightforward, but there are a few things you should know to make sure you're covered no matter where you are.

First off, when it comes to Wi-Fi availability, you'll find that most hotels, resorts, and larger accommodations provide free access to Wi-Fi. In fact, Wi-Fi is generally available in public places like cafes, libraries, shopping centers, and airports as well. I personally used the Wi-Fi in most of my hotels to stay in touch with family and check up on maps and local tips throughout the day. However, there were some more remote areas—particularly on the smaller islands like

Moloka'i or parts of the Big Island—where Wi-Fi service wasn't always available. So, if you plan on venturing into the more secluded parts of the islands, it might be a good idea to either check with your accommodation about internet availability beforehand or be prepared for a little disconnect.

For travelers who need a constant internet connection for work or just want to be able to stay on top of emails and social media, I would recommend bringing a portable Wi-Fi hotspot. There are services that provide portable routers which allow you to connect multiple devices. This option can be especially useful when traveling to remote spots where Wi-Fi access is limited. Another option I explored was picking up a local SIM card for my phone.

If you're coming from the U.S., chances are your phone will work without issues, as long as it's unlocked. I had no problem using my Verizon phone throughout most of the islands. However, if you're visiting from abroad, you may want to buy a local SIM card to save on international roaming fees. The main carriers in Hawaii are T-Mobile, AT&T, and Verizon, and each one has excellent coverage in the more populated areas, like Honolulu or Waikiki. However, if you venture off the beaten path to more rural areas or isolated beaches, some areas may not have the best signal. So, it's important to make sure you're covered before you head off on any adventures.

There are a couple of ways to get a SIM card for your phone when you arrive in Hawaii. Most of the major airports in Hawaii—like Honolulu International Airport (HNL) or Kahului Airport (OGG) on Maui—have kiosks or stores where you can buy a prepaid SIM card. The local mobile providers offer prepaid SIM cards for travelers, which means you won't have to sign a contract or worry about long-term commitments. You can purchase data plans that include talk, text, and internet, which is perfect if you're only in Hawaii for a short period. I found the T-Mobile Prepaid SIM Card to be the best deal for my trip. It gave me unlimited data with good coverage, and I didn't have to worry about tracking my usage. If you want a faster, more reliable option, AT&T also offers 4G LTE service, but I found T-Mobile to be sufficient for my needs.

If you don't want to switch out your SIM card, you can also check if your current carrier offers international roaming or travel plans. For example, Verizon offers international travel plans that allow you to use your phone at the same rates as you would in the U.S. mainland. It's a bit pricier, but it can be an easier option if you don't want to deal with the hassle of changing SIM cards. I ended up sticking with my regular plan and had pretty good reception most places, but I did notice the coverage was a bit spotty in some of the more mountainous or remote regions.

If you're planning to stay connected through apps like WhatsApp, Skype, or any other communication tools, those work just as well in Hawaii as anywhere else. The beauty of modern communication is that you can always stay in touch with people back home or your travel companions no matter where you are on the island, whether through Wi-Fi or cellular data. It also makes booking activities on the go much easier, as many services offer instant messaging or app-based booking.

For anyone heading to Hawaii, my advice is to stay informed about your options for connectivity. While Hawaii is well-equipped with most of the technology you'll need, it's important to know that some remote areas won't have the same level of service. Make sure to plan ahead, especially if you're relying on internet or phone service for work or important communications. If you're unsure about your coverage, check with your carrier before your trip to see if there are any travel packages or SIM cards that can help you get the best experience while you're there.

In the end, while you'll definitely be able to stay connected in Hawaii, the beauty of the islands sometimes lies in stepping away from the phone or computer and embracing the natural surroundings. So, while I loved having the ability to connect when I needed to, I also made sure to take plenty of time to simply disconnect and enjoy the moment.

Language and Useful Phrases in Hawaiian

During my time in Hawaii, I quickly learned that the islands aren't just about beaches and breathtaking landscapes—they also have a language that reflects their deep history and culture. Hawaiian, or 'Ōlelo Hawaii, is a Polynesian language with only 13 letters, but it carries a richness and beauty that is central to the Hawaiian identity. While it's not spoken as widely as English on a day-to-day basis, it's still very much alive in the islands, and you'll find Hawaiian words and phrases used often, especially in place names, signs, and greetings. Even if you don't become fluent, picking up a few key phrases can go a long way in showing respect for the local culture and making your experience feel more connected to the spirit of Aloha.

One of the first things I learned is how important the word Aloha is. It's not just a greeting like "hello"; it carries a much deeper meaning that encompasses love, peace, and compassion. You'll hear it everywhere: when people meet, when they say goodbye, and in all kinds of interactions. So when you step into a store or greet a local, don't be shy—say Aloha! It's a warm and universal way to show you're embracing the culture, even if you're just visiting.

Along with Aloha, another word that became essential to me was Mahalo, which means "thank you." I found myself saying Mahalo to anyone who helped me, from the staff at my hotel to the friendly locals who shared a story or pointed me in the right direction. It's one of those words that immediately makes you feel like you're participating in something greater than just a typical tourist visit—it's a gesture of gratitude that connects you to the Hawaiian way of life.

There's also 'Ohana, which refers to family, but not just the people you're related to by blood. In Hawaii, 'Ohana can also include close friends, neighbors, or anyone with whom you share a strong bond. I found this sense of extended family to be so prevalent in the islands. Everywhere I went, I saw people taking care of each other, and it really made me appreciate the way the Hawaiians view community. When I visited local farms and markets, there was often talk of 'Ohana, whether it was family-run businesses or even just the local pride in sharing the beauty of the island with others. It's not just about individualism; it's about lifting each other up.

As for practical phrases that might come in handy while you're traveling around, there are a few simple ones I used often. For example, if you're looking for directions or want to make sure you're heading in the right place, you can ask, Aia i hea…? which means "Where is…?" It's a great way to strike up a conversation with a local. I used this phrase a lot when trying to find specific places around the island. In return, locals would often share a few directions in Hawaiian, along with the English translation, which made the exchange even more enjoyable.

Another useful phrase that came in handy was 'Ae, which means "yes," and 'A'ole, which means "no." When trying to keep up with conversations in Hawaiian, especially when you're not familiar with all the words, these two simple words will save you a lot of time. When I asked questions about activities or places to eat, locals would sometimes respond with 'Ae or 'A'ole to let me know if they had suggestions or if the place I was looking for was nearby.

If you're visiting during a cultural event or ceremony, you might also hear the word Pono, which means "to be righteous" or "in balance." I found this concept of pono everywhere. Whether it was a traditional hula dance or a meal shared with family and friends, there was a sense of harmony and respect for the land, the sea, and each other. I loved learning that when people use the word pono, they're referring to much more than doing things right—they're talking about living in harmony with everything around you, which is a concept that can apply to all of us, no matter where we come from.

Hawaiian is also present in the names of places. You'll notice that many locations around the islands have long, melodic names. For example, Waikīkī means "spouting waters," and Kauai, the "Garden Isle," is derived from the Hawaiian word kaua'i, which means "a place of abundance." These names are deeply tied to the land, and it's worth taking the time to learn about them. Understanding the meaning behind the names of beaches, parks, and streets can enhance your experience, making it feel more like a connection to the island's history rather than just a passing visit.

Even if you don't master the language, simply using a few Hawaiian words and phrases will be appreciated by the locals. I found that even attempting to speak Hawaiian—though I wasn't perfect—was met with smiles and nods of approval. It's a beautiful gesture that shows respect for the island's traditions and helps to deepen your connection to the people and the land.

If you're curious about the Hawaiian language, I recommend learning a few words before you go, especially if you want to make your visit feel more authentic. While English is widely spoken throughout the islands, learning just a little Hawaiian will show that you care, and it will enrich your experience. To this day, whenever I hear the word Aloha, I smile because it reminds me of the warmth and kindness that Hawaiian culture radiates. It's a reminder that no matter where you come from, you're always welcome in this beautiful place.

CHAPTER 3

Transportation in Hawaii

Getting There: Flights to Honolulu, Maui, Kauai, Big Island, and Other Islands

When I first started planning my trip to Hawaii, one of the first things I had to figure out was how to get there. Hawaii might feel like it's a world away, but thankfully, it's incredibly accessible. Whether you're flying in from the mainland U.S. or internationally, getting to Hawaii is fairly straightforward. The archipelago consists of several islands, each with its own unique vibe and charm. The most common gateway into the islands is Honolulu, located on Oahu, but you can also fly directly into Maui, Kauai, the Big Island, or other smaller islands.

Honolulu is Hawaii's largest city and is located on Oahu, the third-largest island in the archipelago.

It's home to Daniel K. Inouye International Airport (HNL), which is the busiest airport in Hawaii. This makes Honolulu the most common entry point for most travelers. You'll find direct flights to Honolulu from nearly every major airport on the U.S. mainland, including cities like Los Angeles, San Francisco, New York, Chicago, and Seattle. Many international flights also come in here, so if you're traveling from outside the U.S., it's often the first stop. Once you land in Honolulu, you're already in one of the most vibrant, bustling areas in Hawaii, with stunning beaches like Waikiki just a short drive away.

Maui is another popular destination, especially for those looking for a more laid-back, scenic escape. The main airport on Maui is Kahului Airport (OGG), located on the north shore of the island. While you can't find as many direct international flights to Maui, it's fairly easy to get there from Honolulu via a short interisland flight. Flights from cities like Los Angeles, San Francisco, and

Seattle often fly directly into Maui, making it a convenient option if you're traveling from the West Coast.

Kauai, known for its lush landscapes and dramatic coastline, is another island you might want to consider visiting. To get there, you'll fly into Lihue Airport (LIH), which is located on the southeastern coast of the island. While Kauai is less developed than Oahu or Maui, it's still well-connected by air. Many visitors flying from the U.S. mainland typically land in Honolulu first and then hop on a quick interisland flight to Kauai.

The Big Island, as the name suggests, is the largest island in Hawaii. Here, you'll fly into either Ellison Onizuka Kona International Airport (KOA), which is located on the western side of the island, or Hilo International Airport (ITO) on the eastern side. Most visitors arriving from the mainland will land in Kona, which is the island's main hub for tourism. You can easily find direct flights from major West Coast cities like Los Angeles, San Francisco, and San Diego to Kona, making it a popular destination for travelers looking to explore Hawaii's diverse landscapes, including volcanoes, lush rainforests, and beautiful beaches.

Getting to other smaller islands like Lanai, Molokai, or Niihau often requires taking a flight from one of the major islands like Oahu or Maui. These interisland flights are relatively short, typically under an hour, but they provide access to some of Hawaii's more secluded spots. Airlines like Hawaiian Airlines and Mokulele Airlines operate interisland flights, which are generally affordable and easy to book in advance.

One thing I found particularly helpful during my trip was the ease of booking flights in advance. I personally used online booking sites, but I also took advantage of the airlines' websites to monitor any changes in flight schedules or promotions. If you're traveling between islands, it's worth checking out the interisland flights early, as they can sometimes sell out, especially during peak travel seasons.

In my experience, it was easiest to fly directly into Honolulu and then use interisland flights to reach the other islands. The flight times between islands are short, and the views from above are absolutely breathtaking. As I flew from one island to another, I couldn't help but be in awe of the ocean below and the unique landscapes stretching out in every direction. Each island in Hawaii feels distinct, but they're all connected by the same warm, welcoming spirit that makes the Hawaiian Islands so special. Whether you're coming in through Honolulu or landing on one of the other islands, getting to Hawaii is the start of an unforgettable adventure.

Getting Around: Interisland Flights, Local Shuttles, and Rental Options

When it comes to getting around Hawaii, you'll find that there are a number of different options, each tailored to different travel preferences and needs. I remember when I first started exploring the islands, I quickly realized that transportation wasn't quite as simple as just hopping into a car. But as I dug deeper, I discovered the many ways to get around, from interisland flights to rental cars and local shuttles, each offering its own advantages.

Interisland flights are perhaps one of the most convenient ways to travel between the islands. Hawaii's islands are scattered across the Pacific, so it's not always possible to drive from one island to the next. To make these island hops easier, Hawaiian Airlines, Mokulele Airlines, and a few other local carriers offer short, frequent flights between the major islands. These flights are typically under an hour long, and though the prices can vary, they are generally affordable, especially if you book early. For example, a quick flight from Honolulu to Maui might cost you around $70 to $100, depending on when you book and the time of year. I personally found these flights to be super convenient and affordable, and the views from above were nothing short of spectacular.

Flying between islands is particularly handy if you're short on time or if you're planning to visit multiple islands. When I was island hopping during my trip, I opted for interisland flights to move from Oahu to the Big Island and then on to Kauai. These short flights allowed me to maximize my time exploring each island rather than spending hours on the road or ferrying between islands.

For those who prefer not to fly, there are other ways to get around locally on each island. Most islands, especially Oahu and Maui, offer a range of local shuttles and buses that can be both economical and efficient for getting around. Honolulu, the largest city in Hawaii, has a very reliable public bus system called TheBus, which operates throughout Oahu and makes it easy to access major tourist destinations like Waikiki Beach, Diamond Head, and the North Shore. I used TheBus several times during my stay on Oahu and found it to be a straightforward way to get from place to place without worrying about parking or traffic.

On the other islands, while public transportation is available, it's not as widespread as it is in Honolulu. Maui, for example, has a public bus system called the Maui Bus, but it's not quite as comprehensive or frequent. However, there are plenty of shuttle services and taxis that can help you get from point A to point B. If you're staying at a resort, many offer shuttle services that will take you to local beaches, shopping areas, and other popular attractions, which can save you a lot of time and effort if you're not looking to rent a car.

Speaking of rental cars, this is often the go-to option for travelers who want more flexibility and control over their schedules. Hawaii's islands are beautiful, but they're also fairly spread out, so having a car can make all the difference when it comes to seeing all that each island has to offer. Most major airports, including Honolulu (HNL), Kahului (OGG) on Maui, and Kona (KOA) on the Big Island, have rental car services right at the terminal, so you can pick up a car and get going almost immediately. I've rented cars on several islands, and I've found it to be the best way to explore the more remote parts of the islands, like the Hana Highway on Maui or the volcanoes on the Big Island. Be aware, though, that rental prices can fluctuate depending on the time of year, and parking in areas like Waikiki can be pricey and limited.

If you're planning to visit more remote parts of the islands, or if you're looking to explore natural parks and secluded beaches, I highly recommend renting a car. For shorter trips or quick excursions, taxis and rideshare services like Uber and Lyft are readily available in the major cities and towns. These can be especially useful if you don't want the hassle of parking or dealing with long drives.

Overall, the transportation options in Hawaii are designed to give you the flexibility to explore the islands at your own pace. Whether you choose to hop on an interisland flight for a quick getaway to another island or you prefer the comfort and independence of a rental car to explore at your own leisure, there's a transportation solution that will fit your needs. It's all about knowing what works best for you and your itinerary, so you can spend less time worrying about how to get around and more time enjoying everything these islands have to offer.

Navigating Honolulu: Public Transport, Car Rentals, and Taxis

Navigating Honolulu can be a breeze, thanks to the range of transportation options available, but it can also feel a bit overwhelming at first if you're not sure where to start. I remember the first time I landed in Oahu and wondered how I was going to get around this bustling city, especially with so many attractions spread out across the island. Fortunately, Honolulu's transportation system offers a nice variety of choices, whether you prefer public transport, taxis, or the flexibility of renting a car. Let me break down some of the most effective ways to get around Honolulu and make the most out of your time on the island.

First up, public transportation in Honolulu is surprisingly efficient and accessible. TheBus is Honolulu's public transit system, and it's an excellent way to get around the city. It covers not only Honolulu but also the entire island of Oahu, with routes that take you to popular tourist spots like Waikiki Beach, Diamond Head, and the Ala Moana Shopping Center. I personally found TheBus to be reliable and affordable, especially for getting from one part of the city to another. Tickets are around $2.75 per ride, and there are discounted fares for seniors and people with disabilities. You can buy a ticket directly from the driver, or use a reloadable HOLO card, which is available at various retail outlets and vending machines throughout the city.

What I appreciated most about TheBus was its coverage of areas I wouldn't have thought of otherwise. For example, it took me on an unplanned adventure all the way to Pearl Harbor and the Arizona Memorial. The route information is readily available online and at bus stops, and the buses run frequently, so you don't have to wait long to catch one. While TheBus is a great way to get around the main areas, I will say that it might not be the best option if you're planning to visit more remote or less touristy spots on the island.

For those who prefer a more direct and personalized way to get around, taxis and rideshare services like Uber and Lyft are widely available in Honolulu. I've used both during my trips and found them to be quite convenient for getting to places quickly without worrying about parking. There are designated taxi stands at most major hotels, shopping centers, and tourist areas. In addition, rideshare apps are a great option, especially if you're looking to go a bit farther or need a ride at odd hours. I found that rideshare services are usually very efficient in Honolulu, and the drivers are often quite friendly and knowledgeable about the island. Depending on your destination, the fare for a ride within the city can range from $15 to $30.

Now, if you're like me and you love having the freedom to explore at your own pace, renting a car is probably the way to go. While Honolulu has a great public transportation system, nothing beats the flexibility of having your own car when you want to venture off the beaten path. When I rented a car on my last trip to Honolulu, I was able to easily drive around and stop at some of the island's more remote beaches, local parks, and hiking spots without worrying about time constraints or waiting for a bus.

If you're interested in renting a car, there are plenty of rental companies available at the Daniel K. Inouye International Airport (HNL) and throughout the city. Here are a few reputable rental car companies I personally recommend:

Enterprise Rent-A-Car
- **Address:** 300 Rodgers Blvd, Honolulu, HI 96819 (Located at the Honolulu International Airport)
- **Phone:** (808) 836-2727
- **Website:**(http://www.enterprise.com) - - -

- **Price Range:** Rates start from approximately $50-$75 per day, depending on the type of car and season.

Enterprise is known for its friendly service and solid selection of vehicles, including compact cars, SUVs, and luxury options. They also offer free pickup from hotels in certain areas, which can be quite convenient. I rented a compact car here once, and the process was smooth and efficient, with no hidden fees.

Hertz Rent-A-Car
- **Address:** 300 Rodgers Blvd, Honolulu, HI 96819 (Located at the Honolulu International Airport)
- **Phone:** (808) 833-8380
- **Website:** (http://www.hertz.com)
- **Price Range:** Prices start around $40 per day for economy cars, and can go up to $120 for SUVs or specialty vehicles.

Hertz offers a good mix of economy and mid-range cars, along with premium vehicles. I've used Hertz a few times and appreciated their quick and easy process at the airport location. They also have a nice loyalty program if you're planning on renting frequently, and they offer a variety of options including GPS rentals and car seats for families.

Avis Rent-A-Car
- **Address:** 300 Rodgers Blvd, Honolulu, HI 96819 (Located at the Honolulu International Airport)
- **Phone:** (808) 839-3771
- **Website:**(http://www.avis.com)
- **Price Range:** Rates typically start around $45-$65 per day for economy cars.

Avis is another great option if you're looking for a well-known rental brand. They offer reliable vehicles, and their airport location makes it super easy to pick up your car after you arrive. During my trips, I've found their customer service to be solid, and they have convenient options for GPS and additional insurance. Keep in mind that during peak tourist seasons, especially around the holidays or summer, rental prices can rise, and availability can become limited. It's a good idea to book your rental car ahead of time, especially if you plan to rent during the busy season. Additionally, parking in Honolulu, especially in areas like Waikiki, can be expensive and sometimes hard to find. If you're staying in a hotel, check to see if they offer parking, as fees can range anywhere from $20 to $40 per day, depending on the hotel and its location.

Exploring Hawaii: Tips for Island Hopping

Island hopping in Hawaii is one of the most exciting parts of visiting the Aloha State. I remember when I first decided to explore more than just Oahu—I felt like I was in for an adventure, and in many ways, I was. Each island in Hawaii has its own unique charm and character, from the bustling streets of Honolulu to the lush jungles of Kauai, the volcanic landscapes of the Big Island, and the serene beaches of Maui. Getting from one island to the next may seem a bit daunting at first, but with a little bit of planning, it's an incredibly rewarding way to experience the full breadth of what Hawaii has to offer. Let me walk you through some tips that helped me when I was island hopping in Hawaii.

First things first, getting from one island to another in Hawaii is relatively easy thanks to a well-developed network of inter-island flights. The main airlines flying between the islands are

Hawaiian Airlines, Alaska Airlines, and Southwest Airlines. These airlines operate frequent daily flights, and depending on the island, the flights can be as short as 20 minutes (if you're hopping from Oahu to Maui or Kauai) or around 45 minutes (if you're going from Oahu to the Big Island). These flights are affordable too, with one-way fares often starting around $40–$80 if you book early. I've personally used Hawaiian Airlines for most of my inter-island flights, and I was impressed by how smooth the process was—check-in was simple, the planes were comfortable, and the flights were short enough that I could enjoy the view without feeling cramped.

One thing I learned early on was that booking your flights in advance is key. Though these flights are frequent, the demand can increase, especially during peak tourist seasons like summer or the holidays. I once found myself scrambling to get a flight from Maui to the Big

Island during the Christmas season, and I ended up paying more than I had planned. To avoid that, I recommend booking your inter-island flights at least a few weeks ahead of time. Additionally, keep in mind that most of the islands' airports are fairly small, so you won't have to deal with the crowds or the long wait times you'd typically find at major mainland airports.

Now, when it comes to moving around each island, you'll have to think about how you'll get from the airport to your accommodations and how you'll explore once you're there. In many cases, the easiest and most convenient way to get around on the islands is by renting a car. Most airports in Hawaii have a variety of car rental agencies located on-site, and while renting a car can be more expensive than relying on public transportation, it offers the flexibility to explore at your own pace. During my trips, I rented cars from companies like Enterprise, Hertz, and Avis, and it always felt like the best way to get from the airport and venture to the more remote areas. Be sure to compare prices, as rates can vary, and always check if your accommodations offer parking, as finding a space in tourist-heavy areas can be a challenge.

In addition to renting a car, there are also local shuttles and taxis available on most islands. For example, Maui offers a convenient shuttle service from the airport to various tourist areas, and Oahu's Honolulu has a good taxi and ride-sharing scene. While taxis and shuttles are fine for getting to your hotel or certain hotspots, they're not as reliable if you're planning on doing a lot of exploring outside the city centers. If you plan on hiking the lush trails in Kauai or heading to remote beaches on the Big Island, renting a car will give you much more freedom and comfort.

Another tip for island hopping is to keep in mind that each island has its own unique pace and vibe, which can sometimes affect your travel experience. For example, Oahu, especially around Waikiki, is the busiest and most developed, with tons of restaurants, shops, and things to do. If you're hopping from Oahu to the quieter islands like Kauai or Lanai, you'll notice a significant difference in the pace of life. That shift in atmosphere can be quite refreshing, but it also means that some things may not be as easily accessible. On islands like Kauai or Molokai, for instance, there may be fewer rental car options or public transportation routes, so planning ahead is essential.

If you're looking to add a bit of variety to your island hopping experience, you can consider taking a ferry between certain islands. While inter-island flights are the most common way to travel, ferries are a great alternative if you want a slower pace and more scenic views. For instance, there's a ferry that operates between Maui and Lanai, offering travelers a chance to enjoy the ocean breeze while traveling between these two beautiful islands. I took a ferry from Maui to Lanai during one of my trips, and it was a peaceful, relaxed way to make the journey. However, ferry schedules can be less frequent than flights, so it's a good idea to check the timetables ahead of time and make reservations.

When it comes to planning your island-hopping route, it's helpful to think about the experience you want. The islands are all fairly close to each other, but each has its own distinct feel. Oahu, for instance, is perfect for first-time visitors who want to experience the energy of the city along with world-class beaches and shopping. Maui is often considered the "romantic" island, with beautiful beaches, great hiking, and a laid-back vibe. The Big Island is the most diverse, home to active volcanoes, black sand beaches, and otherworldly landscapes. Kauai, known as the "Garden Isle," offers lush rainforests, rugged coastlines, and the most incredible hikes. By planning your route based on what you're looking to experience, you'll be able to hop from island to island in a way that feels meaningful.

One last thing I learned from my island-hopping adventures is that it's worth setting aside time for both the destinations and the journey itself. Sometimes the best part of island hopping isn't just arriving at your next destination but enjoying the stunning views and scenery as you travel. I remember looking out the window of a small plane as I flew from Oahu to the Big Island and thinking how incredible it was to see the vastness of the Pacific Ocean beneath me. The islands of Hawaii are each islands of discovery, and the experience of getting from one to another is an essential part of the magic.

Whether you're traveling to explore new landscapes, experience different cultures, or simply relax on some of the most beautiful beaches in the world, island hopping in Hawaii is an unforgettable experience. With a little bit of planning and a sense of adventure, it's easy to explore multiple islands and make the most of everything this incredible state has to offer.

CHAPTER 4

Accommodation in Hawaii

Luxury Stays: Five-Star Resorts and Boutique Hotels on Major Islands

When I set out to discover the essence of luxury in Hawaii, I quickly learned that the islands cater exquisitely to those seeking high-end experiences. From my own travels, the luxury stays in Hawaii—from five-star resorts to exclusive boutique hotels—are not just about opulence and comfort but also about offering a unique connection to the breathtaking landscapes and rich culture of Hawaii. These establishments are strategically nestled in some of the most stunning locations across the major islands, offering unmatched services, world-class amenities, and an atmosphere that can only be described as paradisiacal.

One of the most renowned luxury resorts that I had the pleasure to stay at is the Four Seasons Resort Maui at Wailea. Located at 3900 Wailea Alanui Drive, Wailea, Maui, HI 96753, this resort is a pinnacle of luxury on Maui. You can reach them at (808) 874-8000 or visit their website at (http://www.fourseasons.com/maui). Nightly rates here can range from $800 to upwards of $10,000 for their most luxurious suites, depending on the season and the specific accommodations. The resort offers everything from serene ocean views and a world-class spa to exquisite dining experiences and private access to Wailea Beach. Their service is impeccable, with a keen attention to detail that makes each guest feel special.

Another incredible destination where I found an exceptional stay was the St. Regis Princeville Resort on Kauai. Located at 5520 Ka Haku Rd, Princeville, Kauai, HI 96722, this resort provides a majestic viewpoint of Hanalei Bay, surrounded by the lush greenery of Kauai's northern shore.

Contact them at (808) 826-9644 or check out their offerings at (http://www.stregisprinceville.com). Room rates usually start around $500 per night and can go much higher for premium suites. The St. Regis boasts a stunning array of amenities including a championship golf course, a native Hawaiian botanical garden, and a spa that offers treatments using local ingredients.

For those who prefer a more intimate setting, the Hotel Wailea in Maui offers a boutique luxury experience that is quite distinct. It is located at 555 Kaukahi Street, Wailea, Maui, HI 96753. Their contact number is (808) 874-0500 and further details can be found at (http://www.hotelwailea.com). This adults-only hotel provides a quieter, more personalized experience. With only 72 suites, each guest receives attentive service and enjoys incredible ocean views. Rates range from $600 to $1,000 per night, providing a luxury experience that focuses on privacy and romantic ambiance.

Oahu also offers its fair share of luxury accommodations, with the Halekulani Hotel being one of the most iconic. Located at 2199 Kalia Road, Honolulu, Oahu, HI 96815, it is known for its gracious hospitality, serene surroundings, and attention to detail. You can contact them at (808) 923-2311 or visit (http://www.halekulani.com) for more information. Prices here vary between $550 to over $3,000 per night, depending on the room or suite. The hotel's oceanfront location and its famed restaurant, La Mer, offer some of the best views and dining experiences in Honolulu. These luxury stays not only provide sumptuous accommodations but also serve as gateways to exploring the rich environment and vibrant culture around them. Each hotel or resort typically offers guided cultural excursions, water sports, golfing, and exclusive tours that can enhance your stay. From personalized hula lessons to helicopter tours over the volcanoes, these experiences are crafted to leave a lasting impression.

Reflecting on my experiences, staying in these luxury hotels and resorts across Hawaii was about more than just enjoying the splendor; it was about immersing myself in the island's natural beauty and cultural heritage in a way that felt both enriching and genuinely respectful of the surroundings. Each stay offered a unique lens through which to view and experience Hawaii, making each moment memorable and each discovery a treasure. Whether waking up to the sunrise over a private beach or enjoying a sunset dinner with locally-sourced ingredients, the luxury accommodations in Hawaii go beyond expectation, offering personalized experiences that are both grand and grounded in local tradition.

Mid-Range Options: Comfortable Hotels and Condos Across Hawaii

When exploring Hawaii on a budget that's generous but not limitless, I discovered a treasure trove of mid-range accommodation options that struck the perfect balance between comfort, convenience, and cost. Whether you're looking for a hotel with all the necessary amenities or a condo that offers a bit more space and a kitchen, Hawaii has plenty of options to choose from that won't break the bank but will still make your stay delightful.

One of my first experiences with mid-range accommodations in Hawaii was at the Aston Waikiki Beach Hotel located at 2570 Kalakaua Avenue, Honolulu, Oahu, HI 96815. You can contact them at (808) 922-2511 or visit their website at (http://www.astonwaikikibeach.com). This hotel is just across the street from Waikiki Beach and offers stunning oceanfront views. The room rates here typically range from $150 to $250 per night, depending on the season and the room type. The hotel boasts amenities such as a pool, on-site dining options, and each room comes equipped with private balconies, giving you a direct view of the ocean or the city. The proximity to the beach and central Waikiki made it extremely convenient for me to explore local shops, restaurants, and nightlife.

For those who might prefer a quieter, more self-sufficient option, I found the Kihei Akahi Condominiums in Maui to be a great choice. Located at 2531 S Kihei Rd, Kihei, Maui, HI 96753, these condos offer a more laid-back atmosphere. Reservations can be made by calling (808) 879-2778 or by visiting (http://www.kiheiakahicondos.com). The condos are priced between $120 and $180 per night. Each unit is equipped with a full kitchen, which was perfect for days when I wanted to cook my own meals. Additionally, the property features two swimming pools, tennis courts, and is just a short walk from Kamaole Beach Park II, a spot that quickly became my favorite for early morning swims and late afternoon sunsets.

On the Big Island, I opted to stay at the Royal Kona Resort situated at 75-5852 Alii Drive, Kailua-Kona, HI 96740. Contact them at (808) 329-3111 or check out their offerings at (http://www.royalkona.com). Room rates here are typically around $170 to $220 per night. The resort sits on the ocean's edge and offers rooms with private lanais, an oceanfront swimming pool, and a luau experience that provides a taste of local culture without having to leave the property. The location was also ideal for exploring the waterfront shops and restaurants of Kailua-Kona. Each of these options provided different experiences tailored to various preferences, from beachfront access and bustling city atmospheres to quiet retreats with room to spread out. Staying in these mid-range accommodations allowed me to enjoy the amenities of higher-end resorts without the steep price tag. It's worth noting that no matter where you choose to stay, booking directly through the hotel or condo's website can often provide you with the best rates and availability, especially during the peak tourist seasons.

Choosing the right place to stay in Hawaii doesn't mean you have to compromise on quality for the sake of affordability. With a range of options from comfortable hotels to cozy condos, you can find the perfect base for your adventures across the islands. These mid-range accommodations are more than just a place to sleep—they are gateways to the experiences and memories that await in the beautiful Hawaiian archipelago.

Budget-Friendly Accommodations: Hostels and Budget Hotels Throughout the Islands

Traveling through Hawaii doesn't have to break the bank, especially when you explore the many budget-friendly accommodations available across the islands. From cozy hostels to affordable hotels, there are options that cater to thrifty travelers who don't want to compromise on the joys of a Hawaiian vacation. During my trips, I discovered several places that offered comfort and convenience without a hefty price tag, and I'd love to share some of these discoveries with you.

One of the standout budget-friendly places I stayed at is The Beach Waikiki Boutique Hostel located at 2569 Cartwright Road, Honolulu, Oahu, HI 96815. It's a gem for travelers looking to stay close to the action without spending a fortune. You can reach them at (808) 922-9190 or check out their offerings at (http://www.thebeachwaikikihostel.com). Nightly rates start as low as $40 for a dormitory room, which is a steal considering its location just a couple of blocks from Waikiki Beach. The hostel offers both private and shared rooms, free Wi-Fi, daily continental breakfast, and organized events like hiking tours and island outings, which are perfect for solo travelers looking to meet new people.

Another great budget option is Maui Beach Hotel, located at 170 Kaahumanu Avenue, Kahului, Maui, HI 96732. Their contact number is (808) 877-0051, and more information can be found on their website (http://www.mauibeachhotel.net). Room rates here can range from $120 to $160 per night, which is quite reasonable for Maui. The hotel offers essential amenities like air conditioning, an outdoor pool, and an on-site restaurant with views of the harbor. Plus, its location in Kahului makes it a convenient base for exploring the island, with easy access to public transportation and the airport.

For those venturing to the Big Island, Kona Seaside Hotel offers great value. It's located at 75-5646 Palani Road, Kailua-Kona, HI 96740, with contact details (808) 329-2455 and online at (http://www.konaseasidehotel.com). Prices here are usually between $130 and $180 per night. This hotel stands out because of its prime location near the oceanfront in Kailua Village, where guests can easily access local shopping, dining, and historical sites. The hotel itself has simple, clean rooms, an outdoor pool, and a garden area that provides a peaceful retreat from the busy downtown area.

If you're headed to Kauai and looking for an economical stay, consider Kauai Palms Hotel. Located at 2931 Kalena Street, Lihue, Kauai, HI 96766, you can call them at (808) 246-0908 or visit (http://www.kauaipalmshotel.com). Rooms here start at about $99 per night. While this hotel offers basic accommodations, it's clean, comfortable, and just a short drive from Lihue

Airport and the Kalapaki Beach. The hotel's friendly staff and cozy atmosphere make it a great choice for budget-conscious travelers.

Each of these accommodations provides not just a place to sleep, but also a friendly environment where you can meet fellow travelers, get local tips, and enjoy a comfortable stay without stretching your budget. I found that staying in these places allowed me more financial freedom to spend on experiences, like helicopter tours over volcanoes, snorkeling excursions, and dining out in local Eateries. Booking directly through the hotel or hostel's website can often secure the best rates, and keeping an eye on travel forums and review sites can help you snag a deal or a last-minute cancellation, especially during the off-peak seasons. Always check what amenities are included to avoid extra charges and consider locations that are central or well-connected by public transport, which can save you money on getting around.

Ultimately, exploring Hawaii on a budget is entirely possible and incredibly rewarding. These budget-friendly accommodations offer not only a place to rest but also an opportunity to deeply immerse yourself in Hawaii's welcoming culture and stunning natural beauty, ensuring your visit is as enriching as it is economical.

Unique Stays: Eco-Resorts, Beachside Bungalows, and Plantation Houses

When I embarked on my Hawaiian adventure, I was keen on experiencing something truly unique, something that went beyond the standard hotel stay. Hawaii, with its rich history and commitment to preserving its stunning natural landscapes, offers an array of unique accommodation options that deeply connect travelers to the spirit of the islands. From eco-resorts nestled in lush greenery to quaint beachside bungalows and historic plantation houses, these unique stays provided an unforgettable experience that was as enriching as it was comfortable.

One of the most memorable places I stayed was the Volcano Rainforest Retreat, located near Volcano Village on the Big Island. Nestled in a lush Hawaiian rainforest near the Volcanoes National Park, this eco-resort is a sanctuary for those looking to immerse themselves in nature. Each of their four cottages is designed with an eco-friendly philosophy, using sustainable materials and practices to minimize their environmental impact. The retreat can be contacted at (808) 985-8696, or you can check out their offerings at (http://www.volcanoretreat.com). Rates range from $250 to $350 per night, depending on the cottage and the season. Staying here, surrounded by the dense, fragrant foliage of the rainforest and the calming sounds of nature, was a profound way to connect with the natural beauty of Hawaii.

For those who dream of waking up to the sound of the waves, the Kauai Beach Bungalows offer a breathtaking escape right on the edge of the water. Located at 4560 Lawai Beach Road, Poipu, Kauai, this small collection of private bungalows provides a serene beachfront experience. Each bungalow is equipped with its own kitchen, which allows for a lovely home-cooked meal by the sea. You can reach them at (808) 742-7588, or visit (http://www.kauaibeachbungalows.com). Nightly rates are typically around $400, which provides value for the prime location and privacy. The proximity to the beach and the inclusion of modern comforts made my stay both relaxing and convenient, offering a gentle, rhythmic soundtrack of ocean waves at night.

Another unique experience is found at the Waimea Plantation Cottages, located on the west shore of Kauai at 9400 Kaumualii Highway, Waimea, HI 96796. This unique property features restored plantation houses that once served as homes for sugar plantation workers. Today, these cottages blend historical charm with modern amenities, creating a peaceful retreat steeped in Hawaiian history. Contact them at (808) 338-1625 or look up their details at (http://www.waimeaplantation.com). Rates start at around $200 per night and can go up to $450 for larger, more luxurious options. Each cottage is distinct, decorated with period furnishings and surrounded by tropical gardens. Staying here felt like stepping back in time, offering a glimpse into Hawaii's plantation past with the comfort of contemporary amenities. These accommodations not only provided a roof over my head but enriched my understanding and appreciation of Hawaii's diverse ecosystems and historical background. They allowed me to live like a local, if only temporarily, and soak in the slower pace of island life. Each place, whether an eco-resort, a beachside bungalow, or a historic plantation house, offered a unique perspective on what it means to truly experience Hawaii.

Choosing where to stay in Hawaii doesn't just come down to finding a place to sleep. It's about finding a place that resonates with your spirit, one that fits the rhythm of your vacation and enhances your connection to this incredible destination.

CHAPTER 5

Culinary Delights Across Hawaii

Traditional and Modern Hawaiian Cuisine

Diving into the world of Hawaiian cuisine was an adventure that tantalized my taste buds and broadened my culinary horizons. From the first time I tasted the traditional flavors to experiencing the modern twists local chefs have infused into their dishes, each meal was a discovery of Hawaii's rich cultural tapestry, portrayed through food.

Traditional Hawaiian cuisine, or what locals might call "local food," has its roots in the native dishes prepared by the original inhabitants of the islands, long before modern influences arrived. The cornerstone of this cuisine is the luau, where dishes like poi—a thick paste made from taro root—and laulau—pork wrapped in taro leaves and steamed—shine as examples of this beautiful simplicity. My first luau was an eye-opening experience into how food can tell the story of a land and its people. The flavors were pure, simple, yet profoundly deep, reflecting the respect for the land that is a big part of Hawaiian culture.

Another traditional dish that captured my heart was poke, which has gained popularity worldwide but is nothing like what I first tried in a small, local market in Honolulu. Traditional poke is typically chunks of raw ahi (tuna) seasoned with sea salt, inamona (a type of roasted crushed kukui nut), and limu (seaweed). Tasting it fresh at the source, where the fish had leapt from the ocean into these simple, delicious dishes, showed me poke in a whole new light. As the islands evolved, so did their cuisine, embracing elements brought by immigrants from Japan, the Philippines, Portugal, and China. This fusion has led to a modern Hawaiian cuisine that is both diverse and delightful. For instance, saimin, a noodle soup that's distinctly Hawaiian, embodies this blend perfectly. It's a dish influenced by Japanese ramen, Chinese mein, and Filipino flavors, which I enjoyed at a quaint eatery in Kauai, where the broth was rich with a depth only centuries of culinary integration could achieve.

In recent years, a new wave of Hawaiian cooking, often referred to as the "Local Food" movement, has emerged, where chefs like Roy Yamaguchi and Alan Wong have pioneered innovative approaches to these traditional recipes, propelling Hawaiian dishes onto the world's culinary stage. For example, Roy's in Honolulu offers a Hawaiian Fusion cuisine that blew me away with dishes that skillfully combine local ingredients like kampachi (amberjack) with Asian-inspired flavors and modern techniques. The modern reinterpretations of Hawaiian cuisine extend beyond restaurants. On my visit to a local farm on Maui, I learned about the farm-to-table concept that many eateries are embracing, highlighting organic local produce and meats in their dishes. Eating at a farm-to-table dinner, where the vegetables on my plate were grown just a stone's throw away from where I sat, added another layer of appreciation for Hawaii's bountiful lands.

Whether you're indulging in a traditional plate lunch of loco moco (rice topped with a hamburger patty, a fried egg, and brown gravy) or dining at upscale restaurants that showcase sophisticated island gastronomy, Hawaiian cuisine offers a palate of flavors that echo its history and herald its future. Each dish not only speaks of the culinary journey of the islands but also tells the story of Hawaii itself—diverse, dynamic, and utterly delicious. Through Hawaiian cuisine, I found more than just food; I discovered a world where every meal is a celebration of life and land. It's a culinary journey that invites anyone who visits the islands to taste, enjoy, and remember the rich cultural heritage that makes Hawaii truly unique.

Regional Specialties by Island

Embarking on a culinary journey through Hawaii reveals not just a universal island cuisine but a delightful array of regional specialties unique to each island. Each dish reflects its environment and history, offering a deep dive into the local culture and traditions through its flavors. As I traveled from one island to the next, tasting my way through local markets and beachside eateries, I was struck by how distinctively the food of each island spoke of its natural resources and the diverse communities that have shaped it.

On Oahu, the bustling street food scene in Honolulu introduced me to poke, but not just any poke. Here, you find innovations like spicy ahi poke or sesame-seared variations that reflect the city's cosmopolitan nature. But Oahu is also renowned for its shave ice, a must-try that's far beyond the typical snow cone. I visited Matsumoto's in Haleiwa, where the finely shaved ice combined with a variety of tropical flavored syrups and a dollop of condensed milk offered a refreshing respite from the island's humid embrace.

Traveling to Maui presented a different palette of flavors, particularly in its use of fresh, local ingredients like the renowned Maui onions, which are sweeter than your average onion and add a subtle crunch and flavor to dishes like the famous Maui onion soup. Another unforgettable treat was the Maui Gold pineapple—a variety that's extra sweet and incredibly juicy. I had the pleasure of tasting this pineapple not just on its own but also in dishes like glazed pork chops and pineapple salsa, which are popular in local taverns and restaurants.

The Big Island, with its vast landscapes and varying climate zones, offers a culinary adventure as large as its geography. Here, coffee reigns supreme, particularly Kona coffee, known worldwide for its rich and robust flavor. Visiting a coffee plantation, I not only sampled this exquisite brew but also learned about the meticulous care that goes into each bean. Additionally, the Big Island is famous for its macadamia nuts. I visited a macadamia nut farm where I sampled everything from roasted nuts to macadamia nut honey—each product a testament to the island's fertile volcanic soil.

Kauai, often called the "Garden Isle," offers specialties that capitalize on its lush landscapes. One of the most memorable meals I had was a traditional taro dish called poi, which is made from the taro root, a staple crop of the islands. In Kauai, they take pride in their ancient methods of cultivating taro in lo'i (wetlands), which I saw firsthand during a cultural tour. The island is also famous for its wild chickens, and while you might see them roaming around, they are also part of traditional dishes like chicken luau, cooked with taro leaves in a creamy, coconut-based sauce.

Each island's culinary offerings provide a taste of the local lifestyle and the natural bounty that Hawaii is blessed with. From Oahu's innovative seafood dishes to Maui's farm-fresh produce, the Big Island's world-class coffee and macadamias, and Kauai's traditional uses of taro, the food here tells the story of Hawaii's diverse cultures and lush land. Dining across these islands isn't just about sustenance; it's about experiencing each island's heart and soul through its most beloved dishes.

Tasting these regional specialties offers more than just culinary delight; it provides insight into the history and culture of each island, making every meal a deeper discovery of what makes Hawaii truly magical. Whether it's your first visit or your hundredth, the islands always have something new and delectable to offer that keeps the spirit of Aloha alive in every bite.

Best Dining Experiences: Top Restaurants and Local Eateries

During my culinary travels across Hawaii, I had the opportunity to dine at some of the most renowned restaurants and local eateries, each offering a unique slice of the islands' rich gastronomic landscape. From high-end dining experiences to casual, family-run spots, the variety and quality of food across the Hawaiian Islands are truly impressive. Here are some of the best dining experiences that stood out during my journey, combining atmosphere, creativity, and, of course, exquisite flavors.

Alan Wong's Restaurant in Honolulu is an absolute must-visit for anyone serious about exploring the finest in Hawaiian regional cuisine. Located at 1857 S King St, Honolulu, this establishment is famed for its innovative approach to local ingredients and flavors. Chef Alan Wong, a pioneer of the farm-to-table movement in Hawaii, crafts dishes that tell a story of the islands' cultural diversity and agricultural bounty. Dining here, I tried the chef's tasting menu, which was a journey through different textures and flavors, each course paired perfectly with exceptional wines. It's a culinary experience that's both refined and deeply rooted in local traditions.

If you find yourself on Maui, make your way to Mama's Fish House in Paia, located at 799 Poho Place. This restaurant is not just a place to eat; it's a destination. Set on a picturesque beachfront, Mama's Fish House delivers a truly authentic Hawaiian seafood experience. The fish served here is caught by local fishermen, with the menu detailing who caught the fish and where, underscoring their commitment to local sourcing. The Polynesian-inspired architecture, the warm, aloha-spirit service, and impeccably fresh dishes, like their signature stuffed fish and tropical fruit-infused cocktails, made my visit unforgettable. For a casual yet quintessentially Hawaiian dining experience, Helena's Hawaiian

Food in Honolulu is unparalleled. Located at 1240 N School St, this eatery is a favorite among locals and tourists alike. Helena's specializes in traditional Hawaiian dishes like pipikaula (dried beef), laulau, and the always comforting kalua pig. Eating here feels like you're part of a Hawaiian family feast—simple, hearty, and extraordinarily flavorful. The atmosphere is unpretentious, with a focus squarely on the food and familial service, which really encapsulates the spirit of aloha.

Over on the Big Island, Huggo's in Kailua-Kona, situated right on the waterfront at 75-5828 Kahakai Rd, offers not just great food but also a stunning view of the Pacific Ocean. Their menu features an array of seafood prepared with a unique Hawaiian twist, and their open-air bar is the perfect spot for a sunset cocktail. The combination of fresh ingredients, the sound of waves crashing, and the tropical breeze made dining at Huggo's a relaxing and memorable experience.

Lastly, if you're up for a culinary adventure, visit Kauai Grill at the St. Regis Princeville Resort on Kauai, located at 5520 Ka Haku Rd. The restaurant offers a sophisticated menu created by acclaimed chef Jean-Georges Vongerichten, focusing on locally-sourced fish and prime meats. The elegant setting and panoramic views of Hanalei Bay add to the luxurious dining experience. Each dish I tried was a testament to culinary craftsmanship, blending global techniques with island flavors.

Each of these establishments not only served extraordinary food but also offered a sense of place and tradition, providing insights into Hawaii's culinary past and present. Whether it was a high-end restaurant or a humble family-run spot, the passion for local ingredients and the pride in Hawaiian culture were evident in every meal. Dining in these places isn't just about food; it's about experiencing Hawaiian hospitality and the islands' love for their land and sea. These experiences are a delicious reminder that great meals can create lasting memories, making them integral parts of any travel experience.

Food Tours and Coffee Plantation Visits

Exploring Hawaii's culinary landscape through food tours and coffee plantation visits was an enriching part of my journey, offering a deeper appreciation for the island's flavors and the people who craft them. These experiences not only tantalized my taste buds but also provided profound insights into the agricultural and culinary traditions that make Hawaii unique.

One of the most memorable parts of my travels was participating in a food tour in Honolulu. These tours are fantastic for any food lover looking to delve into the local cuisine beyond the typical tourist spots. The Oahu Food Tours offer a walking journey through the historic streets of Honolulu, where you can taste everything from traditional Hawaiian dishes to the modern fusion flavors that local chefs are experimenting with today. We sampled everything from poke bowls to shave ice, and each stop included a story about the food's origin and its significance in Hawaiian culture. It was more than a meal; it was a cultural lesson on a plate. The tour guide was incredibly knowledgeable, weaving historical tidbits with culinary insights, making every bite a learning experience.

Another tour took us to the heart of Maui's upcountry, a region known for its farms and rustic landscape. The Maui Farm Tours provide a hands-on approach to understanding the farm-to-table movement that's very prominent in Hawaii. We visited several farms that grow everything from taro to exotic fruits and vegetables. Tasting a freshly picked Maui Gold pineapple, so sweet and juicy, right where it was grown, was nothing short of magical. These tours often end with a meal prepared with ingredients harvested during the tour, offering a taste that's as fresh as it gets. Coffee lovers will find their paradise on the Big Island, home to the world-renowned Kona coffee. Visiting a coffee plantation like Greenwell Farms in Kona can transform your understanding of this beloved brew. Located at 81-6581 Mamalahoa Highway, Kealakekua, these tours are free and walk you through the entire coffee production process—from the coffee fields where the cherries are picked to the roasting process. The highlight, of course, is the coffee tasting. Learning about the climate and volcanic soil that give Kona coffee its distinctive taste adds layers of appreciation to each sip. The sensory overload of smelling fresh coffee while looking over the serene views of the plantation is an unforgettable experience.

Each island offers something unique for foodies. For instance, Kauai, with its lush landscapes, hosts several food tours that focus on local eateries and specialty foods. Tasting Kauai offers tours that introduce you to local restaurateurs and chefs who are pioneering new dishes inspired by traditional Hawaiian ingredients. These experiences are not just about eating; they're about connecting with the people who make the food and understanding their creative processes.

These culinary tours and visits are essential for anyone wanting to see beyond Hawaii's postcard-perfect beaches to its vibrant, flavorful, and innovative culinary heart. Each tour, each meal, and each cup of coffee tells the story of Hawaii's rich cultural tapestry, offering a deeper connection to this beautiful place. Whether you're a foodie or just curious about local cultures, these experiences are sure to enrich your Hawaiian adventure, leaving you with a fuller heart and stomach!

CHAPTER 6

Shopping and Souvenirs in Hawaii

Best Shopping Districts: Honolulu, Lahaina, Kailua-Kona

Navigating the best shopping districts in Hawaii offers a unique blend of traditional and modern retail experiences. From the cosmopolitan streets of Honolulu to the historic charm of Lahaina and the laid-back vibe of Kailua-Kona, each area offers distinct shopping opportunities that are as much about the ambiance and cultural setting as they are about the goods you take home.

Honolulu, on the island of Oahu, is a shopper's paradise. The heart of this district is Ala Moana Center, the world's largest open-air shopping center, located at 1450 Ala Moana Boulevard. This vast mall blends high-end retailers like Louis Vuitton and Chanel with local boutiques that showcase the works of Hawaiian artisans. It's easily accessible by bus or car from anywhere in Honolulu, and offers a comprehensive shopping experience that combines luxury and local flair. Just a short drive away, you'll find the historic district of Waikiki, which is more than just a beach paradise. Kalakaua Avenue, often referred to as the "Fifth Avenue of the Pacific," is lined with both high-end stores and unique Hawaiian shops selling everything from fine jewelry to handcrafted souvenirs. The vibrant street performers and bustling atmosphere make shopping here a lively, engaging experience.

Lahaina on Maui is another must-visit shopping destination, known for its rich history and beautiful oceanfront setting. Front Street is the main thoroughfare, a picturesque stretch along the water where whalers once roamed and now tourists shop. Here, art galleries abound, offering works by local painters and sculptors that reflect the beauty of the islands. Mixed in are shops selling hand-dyed fabrics and clothing unique to Maui. Getting to Lahaina is a scenic drive from most points on the island, with public transportation options available as well. The old Lahaina town atmosphere is palpable as you stroll the ocean-lined streets, making it as much a cultural excursion as a shopping trip.

Kailua-Kona on the Big Island presents a more relaxed shopping vibe but is no less exciting. Ali'i Drive is the main shopping corridor, running parallel to the ocean and dotted with shops that cater to both tourists and locals. Here, you can find specialty stores offering Kona coffee straight from the nearby plantations, local spices, and much more. The area is also famous for its casual, open-air markets where you can pick up fresh local produce and handmade crafts. Kailua-Kona is easily accessible by car and offers ample parking, making it a convenient stop for those exploring the Big Island. Each of these districts provides a window into Hawaii's diverse cultural and commercial landscape, offering more than just products but experiences that resonate with the spirit of Aloha. Shopping in these districts isn't just about what you buy—it's about the memories you create as you explore the sights, sounds, and flavors of Hawaii. Whether you're browsing for high-end fashion in the sophisticated galleries of Honolulu, exploring historical artifacts in Lahaina, or tasting the rich flavors of Kona coffee in Kailua-Kona, you're participating in a tradition of commerce and community that spans the history of the islands. This is where culture meets commerce, and each purchase tells a story of Hawaii's multifaceted identity.

Traditional Hawaiian Goods: Koa Wood, Ukuleles, and Aloha Shirts

Exploring traditional Hawaiian goods is like delving into a rich tapestry of the islands' history, culture, and artistry. Among the most iconic items that represent Hawaii's unique heritage are Koa wood products, ukuleles, and aloha shirts. Each of these items is not just a symbol of Hawaiian culture but also a deep expression of the islands' resources and creativity.

Koa Wood is one of Hawaii's most treasured natural resources, known for its deep rich colors and varied grain patterns. Harvested from the endemic acacia koa tree, which grows predominantly on the higher elevations of the Hawaiian Islands, Koa wood is highly prized for its beauty and the skill required to work it. On a visit to a local woodworker's shop on the Big Island, I learned that Koa was traditionally used to make canoes and surfboards by ancient Hawaiians. Today, it's crafted into more accessible items like bowls, jewelry, and intricately carved sculptures that reflect the island's natural beauty. The warmth of Koa wood items, with their rich hues ranging from deep amber to chocolate browns, carries the essence of the islands' aloha spirit in each piece.

Ukuleles, often synonymous with Hawaiian music, have a joyful sound that seems to capture the light-hearted, melodious spirit of the islands. The ukulele was introduced to Hawaii by Portuguese immigrants in the late 19th century and quickly became an integral part of Hawaiian music culture. In a small, family-run factory in Honolulu, where handcrafted ukuleles are pieced together with native woods like Koa, I discovered just how much craftsmanship goes into each instrument. The ukulele's gentle tones can be heard almost anywhere across the islands, from street performances in bustling Honolulu to serene beachfronts at sunset. Purchasing a ukulele as a souvenir isn't just about taking home a piece of

Hawaiian music; it's about bringing back a soundtrack of your Hawaiian adventures.

Aloha Shirts, also known as Hawaiian shirts, are perhaps one of the most recognizable symbols of Hawaii's laid-back lifestyle and hospitality. Originating in the early 20th century, these shirts were initially made from leftover kimono fabrics and have evolved into a fashion statement with various designs that often feature floral patterns, tropical scenes, and motifs that signify various aspects of Hawaiian life. While exploring the vibrant market scenes in Honolulu, I was drawn to the colorful displays of aloha shirts, each telling a story through its print. From classic, muted designs worn historically by locals for special occasions to the bright, bold patterns that tourists adore, aloha shirts beautifully embody the islands' multicultural history.

Each of these traditional Hawaiian goods — Koa wood, ukuleles, and aloha shirts — offers more than just a memento; they offer a connection to the rich cultural heritage and artistic expression found only in Hawaii. They represent a lifestyle, a history, and a craft that is deeply rooted in the heart of the Pacific. Whether it's the melodious strum of a ukulele, the intricate grain of a Koa wood carving, or the vibrant pattern of an aloha shirt, these items are imbued with the spirit of aloha that makes them timeless symbols of Hawaii. Collecting these items isn't just about shopping; it's about experiencing and appreciating the tangible elements of Hawaiian culture.

Local Markets and Artisan Shops: Handcrafted Goods and Unique Finds

Exploring the local markets and artisan shops in Hawaii is like stepping into a vivid tapestry of creativity and tradition. Each market and shop offers a unique glimpse into the islands' cultural heritage through a variety of handcrafted goods and unique finds that are as diverse as the islands themselves. From bustling farmers' markets to quaint boutiques, these spaces are not just places to shop but are vibrant hubs of local art and craftsmanship.

One of my first and most memorable visits was to the Hilo Farmers Market on the Big Island, located at the corner of Mamo Street and Kamehameha Avenue. Open Wednesday and Saturday, this market is a focal point for both locals and tourists. It's easily accessible by car and there's ample parking nearby, making it a convenient stop for anyone exploring Hilo. Here, you can find everything from exotic fruits and vegetables to handcrafted jewelry, wood carvings, and even locally made soaps. Each stall offers its own slice of Hawaiian life, with artisans eager to share the stories behind their creations. The vibrant atmosphere, fueled by the friendly banter of sellers and the scent of fresh produce, makes for a truly immersive experience.

In Maui, the Lahaina Arts Society Banyan Tree Art Fair under the massive banyan tree in Lahaina is a must-visit. Held during weekends, this art fair gathers some of the best local artists and craftsmen who showcase their work, ranging from photography and paintings to sculptures and handmade crafts. The fair is not only a place to find unique art pieces but also a chance to meet the artists themselves, providing insights into their artistic processes and the inspirations drawn from the beauty of Maui. Getting there is straightforward, as Lahaina is well-signposted and a popular destination for visitors.

For those seeking a more intimate shopping experience, the Na Mea Hawaii in Honolulu offers a wonderful exploration of Native Hawaiian culture through its products. Located in Ward Village, this shop is a treasure trove of traditional Hawaiian books, music, clothing, and crafts. Each item in the store is selected with care, ensuring authenticity and quality. Shopping here is an educational experience, where you can also participate in workshops and talks by local artisans who delve deep into the cultural significance of their crafts.

In Kauai, the charm of small-town shopping comes alive at Hanapepe Town Art Night. Every Friday night, the sleepy town of Hanapepe transforms into a vibrant street festival. Local galleries and shops open their doors late, and artists line the streets with their works. It's a festive environment where you can enjoy live music, great food, and the warm hospitality of Kauai's local community. Hanapepe is located on the south side of Kauai and is easily accessible by car from Poipu or Lihue, making it a lovely evening getaway.

Each visit to these markets and shops offered me not just souvenirs to bring back home but stories and memories of the people behind them. The dedication to craft and community spirit is palpable, making every item purchased a direct support to the local economy and a nod to preserving the rich cultural heritage of Hawaii. Whether you're searching for a unique gift or a piece of Hawaiian culture to bring home, the local markets and artisan shops across the islands provide a diverse and enriching shopping experience that goes beyond the ordinary.

CHAPTER 7

Nightlife and Entertainment in Hawaii

Vibrant Nightlife: From Honolulu Clubs to Maui Beach Bars

Exploring the vibrant nightlife of Hawaii has been one of the highlights of my travels through the islands. From the bustling nightclubs of Honolulu to the laid-back beach bars of Maui, each locale offers a unique experience that reflects the island's personality and caters to both residents and visitors alike.

In Honolulu, the nightlife is as dynamic and diverse as the city itself. The heart of the action can be found in the bustling district of Waikiki. Here, nightclubs like The Republik offer a sleek, modern environment where local and international DJs spin the latest hits, drawing a lively crowd that dances well into the night. Located at 1349

Kapiolani Blvd, The Republik is easily accessible by bus, taxi, or a short walk from many of the major hotels, making it a convenient option for those looking to experience Honolulu's nightlife.

Another hotspot is Addiction Nightclub at The Modern Honolulu, where the city's glamorous come to see and be seen. With its chic decor and pulsating music, Addiction offers a taste of Honolulu's upscale nightlife scene. It's located at 1775 Ala Moana Boulevard, just a quick taxi ride from downtown, providing an ideal locale for tourists staying in the area who are eager to experience a night of luxury and excitement. Meanwhile, over on Maui, the nightlife shifts gears towards a more relaxed vibe, with beach bars that offer a perfect blend of tropical cocktails and stunning sunset views. Moose McGillycuddy's in Lahaina is a favorite among locals and tourists alike. Situated at 844 Front St, this bar provides a casual atmosphere where you can enjoy live music, dance, and dine under the stars. The beachfront location makes it a scenic spot to unwind after a day of exploring Maui.

Not far from Lahaina, you'll find Charley's Restaurant and Saloon in Paia, known for its laid-back atmosphere and frequent live music performances. As a favorite haunt for local musicians and visitors, Charley's, located at 142 Hana Highway, offers a rustic charm that is quintessentially Maui. It's a place where you can sip on a local brew, listen to some of the best live bands on the island, and even catch impromptu performances by visiting celebrities. Both Honolulu and Maui offer distinct nightlife experiences that cater to different tastes—whether you're looking for a high-energy dance club or a serene spot by the sea to enjoy a cocktail. Navigating through these areas is quite straightforward. In Honolulu, public transportation and taxis are readily available, making it easy to hop from one venue to another.

In Maui, renting a car might be preferable if you plan on exploring various spots along the coast.

What truly makes Hawaii's nightlife special is not just the variety of venues but the warm, welcoming nature of the people. Whether you're dancing the night away in a club in Honolulu or enjoying a mai tai at a beach bar in Maui, the friendly spirit of Aloha permeates every experience, making each night out feel like a celebration of island life. As someone who has enjoyed countless evenings under the Hawaiian sky, I can attest that the islands offer some of the most memorable nightlife experiences in the world.

Live Music and Traditional Hawaiian Hula Shows

Immersing oneself in Hawaii's live music and traditional hula shows is akin to stepping into a vivid narrative that captures the islands' heart and soul. These performances are more than entertainment; they are vibrant expressions of Hawaii's rich cultural heritage and history.

One of the most unforgettable experiences I've had was attending a live hula show. Hula, more than just a dance, is a powerful form of storytelling, where every movement and expression conveys a piece of Hawaii's history and the aloha spirit. The Old Lahaina Luau on Maui provides an authentic hula experience that is deeply rooted in tradition. Located at 1251 Front Street in Lahaina, getting there is easy by car or taxi, and it's well worth planning an evening to enjoy this cultural feast. The luau starts with a traditional Hawaiian feast, followed by a hula performance under the stars. The dancers, adorned in traditional costumes, perform to the sounds of live Hawaiian music, making it a mesmerizing experience that resonates with the tales of the islands.

For those interested in more contemporary live music, Hawaii's local bars and resorts often feature talented local musicians who bring a modern twist to traditional Hawaiian sounds. In Waikiki, Duke's Canoe Club offers live music nightly, with a beachfront setting that enhances the experience. Located at 2335 Kalakaua Ave., Duke's is a prime spot for enjoying the soothing sounds of contemporary Hawaiian music while sipping a tropical cocktail and watching the sunset over the Pacific. On the Big Island, the Kona Brewing Company at 74-5612 Pawai Place in Kailua-Kona not only serves up locally crafted beers but also hosts live music performances that feature a blend of Hawaiian and contemporary styles. The laid-back atmosphere, combined with great music and even better beer, provides a perfect backdrop for a relaxing evening.

Visiting these venues offers a glimpse into the heart of Hawaiian music and dance culture. Each performance, whether traditional hula or a band playing modern Hawaiian tunes, provides a connection to the islands' traditions and a deeper understanding of the diverse cultural influences that shape contemporary Hawaiian music. These live music and hula performances are essential for anyone wanting to experience Hawaii's vibrant cultural scene. Each event is a celebration of life and the enduring spirit of the islands, showcasing talents that continue to inspire awe and respect for Hawaii's rich artistic heritage. Whether it's through the graceful storytelling of hula or the harmonious blend of modern and traditional sounds, the music and dance of Hawaii provide a profound sense of place that stays with you long after the night ends.

Best Bars and Entertainment Venues Across the Islands

Diving into the nightlife across the Hawaiian Islands reveals a spectrum of bars and entertainment venues that cater to every preference, from laid-back beachfront spots to bustling, upbeat bars. Each venue offers a unique ambiance that perfectly complements its locale, providing both residents and visitors with unforgettable nights out under the stars or beneath the neon lights.

Starting off in Honolulu, the Mai Tai Bar at the Ala Moana Center (1450 Ala Moana Blvd) is an iconic destination. Known for its award-winning cocktails and live music, it offers a vibrant outdoor setting that captures the lively spirit of Oahu. The bar overlooks the beautiful Pacific Ocean, providing a scenic backdrop to enjoy some of the best live bands that play contemporary and traditional Hawaiian music. The Mai Tai Bar is easily accessible by public transportation or car, with ample parking in the Ala Moana shopping complex.

Over on Maui, Mulligan's on the Blue in Wailea (100 Kaukahi St) is a favorite for both locals and visitors. This Irish pub with a Hawaiian twist overlooks the stunning Wailea Old Blue Golf Course and offers a hearty mix of live music, ranging from local Hawaiian to traditional Irish tunes. Getting there is a breeze with a short drive from most major resorts in Wailea, and there's plenty of parking on site. The pub's lively atmosphere is perfect for a night of dancing and dining under the Maui sky. On the Big Island, Huggo's on the Rocks in Kailua-Kona (75-5828 Kahakai Rd) is the ultimate beach bar experience. Just steps away from the ocean, this bar is renowned for its casual, sandy-floored setting and live Hawaiian music. The casual menu, featuring fresh, local seafood and tropical drinks, complements the laid-back vibe. It's a fantastic spot to watch the sunset and even catch sight of manta rays cruising along the coast. Huggo's on the Rocks is a short walk from Ali'i Drive's main strip, making it a convenient stop during a night out in Kailua-Kona.

Kauai offers a more intimate nightlife experience at Rob's Good Times Grill in Lihue (4303 Rice St). Known as Kauai's premier sports bar, Rob's features karaoke nights and live bands that play a wide variety of music from rock to reggae. The venue is just a short drive from the Lihue Airport and nearby hotels, making it an easy choice for an evening out in Kauai. With multiple screens to watch sports games and a lively local crowd, it's a great place to mingle with residents and tourists alike. Each of these bars and venues offers more than just drinks and music; they provide a gateway to the cultural and social heartbeat of Hawaii.

CHAPTER 8

Oahu: The Heart of Hawaii

Exploring Oahu is like stepping into a living postcard, where vibrant geographic features and a mild, welcoming climate are just the beginnings of the island's allure. Through my travels across this stunning island, I've come to understand how deeply Oahu's geography, climate, and rich history are intertwined, each shaping the experiences of everyone who visits.

Oahu, known as "The Gathering Place," is the third largest of the Hawaiian Islands, but it's number one in population. The island's geography is a dynamic spectacle of nature, characterized by two major mountain ranges— the Waianae range to the west and the Koolau range to the east. These volcanic mountains frame a central plain that's a hub of agricultural activity, ensuring that the island isn't just a place of scenic beauty but also of bountiful produce. Between these ranges, the island dips into valleys and rises into majestic peaks, such as the iconic Diamond Head, an extinct volcanic crater that stands guard over Honolulu. The coastlines of Oahu are equally dramatic, with the North Shore known worldwide for its towering winter waves, making it a mecca for surfers globally.

The climate here is as pleasant as you might imagine in a tropical paradise—mostly sunny, with temperatures that rarely dip below 65°F (18°C) or rise above 89°F (32°C). This consistent weather, marked by passing showers that quickly give way to rainbows, makes Oahu a year-round destination for tourists and a joyful place for locals to live. The island's climate also supports diverse ecosystems, from the lush, rain-soaked valleys like Manoa to the drier, leeward coasts, offering a variety of experiences to nature lovers. The rich history of Oahu is a tapestry that's as colorful as its landscapes. The island was the home of the Hawaiian monarchy, and it's where you'll find Iolani Palace, the only royal palace in the United States. This historical gem in downtown Honolulu isn't just a museum; it's a national historic landmark that tells the story of the Hawaiian Kingdom.

In more recent history, Pearl Harbor, located just west of Honolulu, marks a pivotal moment not just for Oahu but for the world, as the site of the 1941 attack that drew the United States into World War II. Visiting the USS Arizona Memorial offers a poignant glimpse into this significant event, providing context and reflection on its global impact. The convergence of geography, climate, and history on Oahu creates a living environment where the past and present coexist beautifully.

Waikiki Beach, Pearl Harbor, Diamond Head

Visiting Oahu's major attractions like Waikiki Beach, Pearl Harbor, and Diamond Head offers a blend of scenic beauty, somber history, and adventurous exploration that truly encapsulates the spirit of Hawaii.

Waikiki Beach is perhaps the most famous beach in Hawaii, known for its golden sands and azure waters that stretch along the south shore of Honolulu. The beach is not only a paradise for sunbathers and swimmers but also serves as a prime location for beginners in surfing due to its gentle waves. Access to Waikiki is effortless with numerous public transport options, ample parking, and a variety of walking paths. Strolling along the Kalakaua Avenue that borders the beach, you're immersed in a vibrant atmosphere of live music, street performers, and local eateries that capture the lively spirit of Oahu. My personal experience watching the sunset from Waikiki, with the silhouette of Diamond Head in the distance, was nothing short of magical.

Pearl Harbor, located a short drive west of Honolulu, is a must-visit for its profound historical significance. The site of the December 7, 1941, attack that brought the U.S. into World War II is now home to several memorials, including the USS Arizona Memorial. Visitors can take a boat ride to the floating memorial directly above the sunken battleship, where oil still seeps from its remains, a poignant reminder of the lives lost. The Pearl Harbor Visitor Center and the surrounding museums offer exhibits that provide deeper insights into the events of World War II and its lasting impacts. Reaching Pearl Harbor is straightforward by car, bus, or guided tours, which are readily available from most parts of the island.

Diamond Head, an iconic landmark east of Waikiki, offers a different kind of adventure. This massive volcanic tuff cone is visible from almost anywhere in Honolulu and is a popular hiking destination that promises panoramic views of the Pacific Ocean and Honolulu. The trail to the summit is well-maintained, though somewhat steep, and takes about 40-60 minutes to climb. My ascent of Diamond Head was exhilarating, filled with historical tidbits along the way, such as old military bunkers and a navigation lighthouse at the summit. The view from the top, overlooking Waikiki and the vast ocean, is truly rewarding.

Each of these attractions not only offers visitors a chance to experience the natural beauty and historical depth of Oahu but also brings to life the stories and heritage of Hawaii. Whether you're surfing the gentle waves of Waikiki, reflecting on the history at Pearl Harbor, or climbing the storied slopes of Diamond Head, these sites provide a profound sense of place and history that is deeply moving and uniquely Hawaiian.

Hidden Gems: Manoa Falls, Chinatown Arts District

Exploring Oahu reveals some truly remarkable hidden gems that go beyond the well-trodden paths, offering serene escapes and cultural depth that can transform an ordinary visit into a memorable adventure. Two such places are Manoa Falls and the Chinatown Arts District, each providing a unique glimpse into the island's diverse landscapes and vibrant cultural scene.

Manoa Falls is nestled in the lush Manoa Valley, just a short drive from the bustling streets of downtown Honolulu. This hike, suitable for all ages and fitness levels, leads to a breathtaking 150-foot waterfall. The trail is a relatively easy 1.6 miles round trip but is a world away from the city's hum. As you walk through the verdant rainforest, the air fresh with the scent of tropical flowers and the sounds of birds and streams around you, it feels like stepping into another world. The path can be muddy and slippery, so wearing proper footwear is advisable. Getting to the trailhead is straightforward, with several public buses leading to Manoa Valley, and parking available near the entrance for those driving. My own journey to the waterfall was as enchanting as the destination itself, with every step revealing the rich, green beauty that makes Manoa Falls a must-visit for nature lovers.

Chinatown Arts District, located in the heart of Honolulu, presents another facet of Oahu's charm. This vibrant neighborhood is a stark contrast to the serene trails of Manoa. Known for its historical architecture, eclectic shops, and bustling markets, Chinatown is also a booming arts hub. During the day, the streets are alive with marketgoers and local artisans selling their crafts. By night, the area transforms into a lively cultural scene with galleries, theaters, and bistros hosting live music and art events. One of my favorite experiences was attending a First Friday, a monthly event where galleries and studios open their doors late into the evening, offering a festive atmosphere with art installations, street performers, and food vendors. Access to Chinatown is easy via public transport or by car, with ample parking in municipal lots.

Both Manoa Falls and the Chinatown Arts District showcase the diversity of experiences available on Oahu. Whether you're a nature enthusiast eager to explore the lush landscapes of Hawaii or a culture seeker looking to dive into the artistic heart of Honolulu, these destinations provide enriching experiences that resonate long after your visit ends. Each location offers not just sights to see, but stories to engage with, making them essential stops on any Oahu itinerary.

Hiking in the Ko'olau Range, Surfing in the North Shore

Experiencing Oahu's outdoors is truly about embracing the island's natural elements, from its lush mountain ranges to its legendary surf breaks. As someone who loves both hiking and surfing, exploring the Ko'olau Range and tackling the waves on the North Shore have been highlights of my adventures in Hawaii.

Hiking in the Ko'olau Range offers some of the most breathtaking views on Oahu. The range stretches along the eastern side of the island, providing a dramatic backdrop to Honolulu. One of the most accessible and rewarding trails is the Lanikai Pillbox Hike, which starts near Kailua. The trailhead is easy to find, with local signage directing hikers to the starting point, accessible by car or bus from downtown Honolulu. The hike itself is moderately challenging, involving some steep sections, but it's absolutely worth it. Reaching the old military pillboxes at the top, you're greeted with a panoramic view of the windward coast, including the stunning Lanikai Beach and the Mokulua Islands. The early morning hike to watch the sunrise from the pillboxes is something I'll never forget—the colors and the serene ocean view were simply mesmerizing.

Surfing in the North Shore is an entirely different kind of thrill. Known globally as the surfing capital of the world, the North Shore transforms during the winter months when the waves become monumental, drawing surfers from across the globe. Towns like Haleiwa serve as the hub for surf enthusiasts, and the vibe is infectious. For beginners, summer is the best time to visit, as the waves are much smaller and manageable. Surf schools dot the coastline, offering lessons for all levels. I took my first surfing lesson here, and there's nothing quite like the rush of catching your first wave. The power of the ocean beneath you, the taste of salt in the air, and the sheer joy of riding along the water's surface—it's an exhilarating experience that embodies the spirit of Oahu.

Both activities highlight the contrasts and the balance of Oahu's outdoor offerings—whether you're seeking tranquility atop a mountain or adrenaline on the waves. Each adventure is deeply connected to the natural beauty of the island, offering not just physical challenges but also spiritual rejuvenation. What makes Oahu special is this blend of mountain and sea, providing endless opportunities for outdoor enthusiasts to connect with nature in profound and exhilarating ways.

Shave Ice, Poke Bowls

Exploring the culinary delights of Oahu, particularly shave ice and poke bowls, is akin to taking a flavorful journey through the island's vibrant food culture. These two iconic dishes offer a taste of local tradition and modern culinary creativity, each telling a story of Hawaii's multicultural influences.

Shave Ice is not just a treat; it's a must-have experience when visiting Oahu. One of my first stops was the famous Matsumoto Shave Ice in Haleiwa on the North Shore, a place that's almost become a pilgrimage site for this icy delight. Here, shave ice is served up with a craftsmanship that respects the simplicity yet potential complexity of the dessert. Starting with a block of ice finely shaved into a snow-like texture, it's then generously doused with a variety of syrups ranging from traditional tropical flavors like mango and passionfruit to more inventive ones like green tea or sweetened condensed milk. The result is a refreshing, melt-in-your-mouth flavor explosion that's both cooling and invigorating on a warm Hawaiian day. What makes Matsumoto's stand out is the option to add a scoop of ice cream at the base, transforming each bite into a creamy delight. The process of watching it being made is as much a part of the experience as tasting it, with each layer skillfully added to create a colorful and flavorful masterpiece.

Poke Bowls, on the other hand, are a testament to Hawaii's rich sea-centric culture. My introduction to authentic Hawaiian poke came at Ono Seafood in Honolulu, known for its fresh, high-quality fish. Poke, which means "to slice" in Hawaiian, typically features cubes of raw fish—usually tuna—marinated in a variety of seasonings. At Ono Seafood, the traditional poke bowl includes options like soy sauce, green onions, and sesame oil, which highlight the fish's fresh flavor without overpowering it. Other variations might include sweet onions, seaweed, or even spicy mayo, catering to a range of palates. Sitting down with a poke bowl in Oahu, with its direct access to some of the freshest fish in the world, is about appreciating the simplicity and freshness of the ingredients—something that's deeply ingrained in Hawaiian culinary practice.

Each of these dishes provides a window into the heart of Oahu's culinary scene, reflecting the island's history, culture, and modern-day lifestyle. Shave ice and poke aren't just food; they're cultural icons, embodying the spirit of Aloha that is so pervasive here. They invite locals and visitors alike to pause and savor life's simpler pleasures, each bite a reminder of the islands' lush beauty and vibrant community. Whether it's the sweet, chilled layers of a shave ice or the rich, savory depth of a poke bowl, these experiences are fundamental to understanding and enjoying what Oahu has to offer.

Luxury Resorts, Surf Hostels

Staying in Oahu offers a delightful spectrum of accommodations, from the heights of luxury at grand resorts to the laid-back vibes of surf hostels. Each option provides a unique way to experience the island, catered to different tastes and travel desires.

Luxury Resorts in Oahu are synonymous with indulgence and high-class service. The Halekulani Hotel, located at 2199 Kalia Road in Honolulu, is a prime example of opulence in paradise. Renowned for its impeccable service, elegant rooms, and stunning views of Waikiki Beach, the Halekulani lives up to its name, meaning "House Befitting Heaven." Room rates typically range from $500 to over $1,000 per night, depending on the season and room type. Guests can enjoy amenities like an oceanfront spa, a fitness room, and a heated pool overlooking the sea, not to mention dining at La Mer, one of Hawaii's top-rated restaurants. Contacting the hotel is easy via their website (http://halekulani.com) or by phone at (808) 923-2311.

For those looking for a more immersive surf experience, Surf Hostels offer a budget-friendly, community-oriented lodging option. The Backpackers Vacation Inn and Plantation Village located at 59-788 Kamehameha Highway in Haleiwa is a perfect spot for those who want to catch the famous North Shore waves. Nightly rates here are much more affordable, typically ranging from $35 for a dormitory-style room to around $150 for private accommodations. This hostel provides simple amenities, including access to a communal kitchen, Wi-Fi, and, most importantly, a prime location near some of the world's most famous surf spots. More details and booking options can be found on their website (http://backpackershawaii.com) or by calling (808) 638-7838. Choosing between these types of accommodations depends largely on what kind of experience you're seeking in Oahu. If it's luxury and tranquility, surrounded by world-class services, then a resort like the Halekulani will not disappoint. On the other hand, if you're after adventure and the chance to meet fellow travelers, then staying at a place like Backpackers Vacation Inn will place you right in the heart of the surfing culture.

Both options provide excellent bases from which to explore the island. The luxury resorts offer tours and excursions directly from their concierges, making it easy to see the island's sights without needing to plan too much on your own. Surf hostels, meanwhile, often organize group activities and outings, which not only help you see the island but also build friendships along the way. No matter where you choose to stay, Oahu's range of accommodations ensures that you can find the perfect spot to relax after a day full of exploring everything the island has to offer—from sun-soaked beaches and scenic hikes to local eateries and vibrant marketplaces. Each night's stay, whether ensconced in luxury or cozied up in a surfer's bungalow, adds its own rich layer to your Hawaiian adventure.

Sunset Cruises, Luau Experiences

Experiencing the nightlife and entertainment in Oahu provides a perfect blend of scenic beauty and cultural richness, and two of the most quintessential activities are sunset cruises and luau experiences. Both offer unique ways to enjoy the island's natural allure and hospitable culture in settings that are as breathtaking as they are enjoyable.

Sunset Cruises off the coast of Oahu are magical. I remember boarding a catamaran from Waikiki Beach, just as the sun began its descent into the Pacific. The sky turned a palette of pink, orange, and purple, colors so vivid they seemed unreal. Most sunset cruises can be accessed from major points along Waikiki and range in price from $50 to $100 per person, depending on the amenities offered, such as live music or dinner. These cruises not only offer stunning oceanic views but also a chance to see Honolulu's skyline from a different perspective. The gentle sway of the boat, the sound of the ocean against the hull, and the silhouette of Diamond Head in the distance create a truly enchanting evening. It's a perfect setting for a romantic outing or a peaceful moment to reflect on the beauty of Hawaii.

Luau Experiences in Oahu are not to be missed for those looking to dive deeper into Hawaiian culture. The luau is a traditional Hawaiian party or feast that features entertainment like hula dancing and fire performers, and it's often accompanied by a meal of traditional Hawaiian food like poi, kalua pig, poke, and haupia. One of the most immersive luaus I attended was the Polynesian Cultural Center's Ali'i Luau located at 55-370 Kamehameha Hwy in Laie. It offers a comprehensive experience that starts with a tour of the historic Polynesian villages, followed by the luau and a breathtaking evening show titled "Ha: Breath of Life," which tells a Polynesian saga with dancers, fire performers, and music. Prices for these experiences vary but generally start around $100 per person, which includes entry to the center, the luau, dinner, and the show.

These sunset cruises and luau experiences encapsulate the essence of Oahu's nightlife and entertainment, offering more than just fun; they offer a pathway to understanding and appreciating the island's scenic and cultural landscapes. Whether you're toasting to a beautiful sunset aboard a cruise or feasting and celebrating at a luau, these activities highlight the warmth and beauty of Oahu, making any evening unforgettable. Through these experiences, I not only held on to moments of beauty but also gained deeper insights into what makes Oahu truly special—the blend of its natural wonders with its rich traditions.

CHAPTER 9

Maui: The Valley Isle

Exploring Maui, often called "The Valley Isle," unfolds a breathtaking array of landscapes that narrate a story as rich and deep as the Pacific Ocean that embraces its shores. During my explorations across Maui, I've become intimately acquainted with its distinct geography, diverse climate, and rich history, each element revealing part of what makes this island truly captivating.

Maui's geography is dramatically diverse, characterized by its two major volcanic regions separated by a verdant isthmus. The older West Maui Mountains, with their deeply eroded peaks and lush valleys, tell tales of a volcanic past long settled. In contrast, Haleakala, the massive shield volcano that dominates East Maui, rises majestically to over 10,000 feet. Its summit offers some of the most stunning sunrises in the world—viewing the sunrise from Haleakala's peak is an ethereal experience that feels like watching the world wake up. The island's coastline varies from the famous golden sands of Kaanapali Beach in the west to the rugged, untamed shores of Maui's eastern coast.

Maui's climate varies almost as much as its geography. The island's leeward western and southern sides enjoy a drier, sunnier climate, which makes them popular for resorts and beach activities. Conversely, the windward eastern side receives more rainfall, creating lush landscapes that are a hiker's and nature lover's paradise. This climatic diversity allows for spectacular driving adventures, notably the Road to Hana, where each turn along the winding road offers a new microclimate and view, from rainforests and waterfalls to panoramic ocean vistas. The rich history of Maui is as layered as its soil. The island was once a chiefdom in ancient Polynesia, ruled by the legendary Piilani line. In the late 18th century, King Kamehameha I conquered Maui as part of his campaign to unify the Hawaiian Islands, a pivotal moment in Hawaii's history that led to the formation of the Kingdom of Hawaii. The island also played a significant role during the whaling era in the mid-19th century, with Lahaina serving as an important global whaling port. This historic town remains a window into the past, with preserved buildings and museums like the Baldwin Home Museum offering glimpses into 19th-century life.

Understanding Maui's geography, climate, and history enhances the experience of visiting this diverse island. Whether hiking through Iao Valley's lush trails, watching whales breach off the coast during migration season, or exploring historic Lahaina town, you're constantly reminded of the rich tapestry of natural and human history that weaves together to form Maui's unique cultural and environmental identity.

Road to Hana, Haleakala National Park

Exploring Maui's Road to Hana and Haleakala National Park are experiences that encapsulate the breathtaking diversity of the island's natural landscapes. Both journeys offer unique adventures that are fundamental to understanding the essence of Maui.

The Road to Hana is more than just a drive; it's a journey through a lush, vivid showcase of Maui's natural beauty. Starting from Kahului, the route covers about 64 miles of narrow, winding roads that lead to the small town of Hana. This drive is famous not just for its final destination but for the incredible sights along the way. With over 600 curves and more than 50 one-lane bridges, the road takes you through dense rainforest, past cascading waterfalls, and alongside stunning coastal views. Highlights include the Keʻanae Peninsula, offering jaw-dropping views of the rugged coast against the backdrop of pounding surf, and Waiʻanapanapa State Park, where you can explore a black sand beach, sea caves, and ancient lava tubes. The journey typically takes a full day, considering stops for sightseeing, swimming, and enjoying roadside stands with fresh fruit and local snacks. Reaching the start of the Road to Hana from Kahului is straightforward, as it begins right at the town's outskirts. Most visitors drive themselves, which allows for a flexible itinerary, though numerous guided tours are available that provide insights into the area's history and ecology not immediately obvious to the uninitiated eye.

Haleakala National Park, on the other hand, offers a stark contrast to the lush tropical scenery of the Road to Hana. The park is centered around Haleakala Crater, the largest dormant volcano in the world. Visiting this national park provides a glimpse into a stark, almost otherworldly landscape. Ascending to the summit of Haleakala, particularly for sunrise, is a sacred and awe-inspiring experience that many describe as spiritual. The summit area's elevation at over

10,000 feet can bring subfreezing temperatures and rapidly changing weather, but it also offers panoramic views that stretch across the entire island and beyond. For the adventurous, Haleakala offers extensive hiking trails that descend into the crater, revealing a landscape of cinder cones and rare native plants.

Access to Haleakala National Park is via Highway 37 to 377 and finally 378. The drive from Kahului to the summit takes about two hours. It is advisable to arrive early, as sunrise viewings are extremely popular and now require reservations due to their popularity. Both the Road to Hana and Haleakala National Park not only showcase Maui's stunning natural beauty but also provide visitors with profound connections to the island's raw, powerful landscapes. These experiences, from coastal to volcanic, ensure that Maui holds a place in the hearts of those who travel its breadth, leaving memories that linger long after the journey ends.

Upcountry Distilleries, Paia Town

Exploring Maui's Upcountry and the quaint town of Paia offers some of the island's most charming and less trodden experiences. Nestled in the lush, rolling hills of Maui's Upcountry are several distilleries that exemplify the spirit of the island—quite literally—with locally sourced ingredients and unique distillation processes.

Upcountry Distilleries like the Hali'imaile Distilling Company have carved a niche by using local ingredients in their spirits. Located at 883 Haliimaile Road, this distillery is famed for its Pau Maui Vodka, distilled from pineapples sourced from the nearby fields but without the fruit's sweetness, yielding a pure, clean spirit. A visit here offers an in-depth look at their process, from fermentation to distillation, often ending with a tasting session that reveals the subtleties of flavor that only local ingredients can provide. Tours and tastings can be booked online via their website (http://www.haliimailedistilling.com) or by phone at (808) 883-2080, with prices for tours starting around $10 per person. Just a short drive from these distilleries is Paia Town, a gem on Maui's north coast. Known for its bohemian vibe and picturesque setting, Paia is a haven for surfers, artists, and visitors looking for a laid-back atmosphere. Walking through Paia, with its colorful boutiques and casual eateries, feels like stepping back in time.

When it comes to dining and staying in Paia, there are delightful options that cater to all tastes and budgets. Paia Inn, located at 93 Hana Highway, is a boutique hotel right in the heart of town. This small but elegant hotel offers a beachy, modern decor, private beach access, and a central location perfect for exploring local shops and restaurants. Room rates range from $200 to $400 per night, depending on the season and room type. Contact details and reservations can be made through their website (http://paiainn.com) or by phone at (808) 579-6000.

For dining in Paia, Mama's Fish House is an iconic stop. Located just outside Paia at 799 Poho Place, this restaurant is famous not only for its exquisite seafood dishes but also for its commitment to local fishermen and fresh ingredients. The atmosphere is pure Polynesia, with stunning views of the ocean. Dining here is a bit of a splurge with entrees ranging from $50 to $60, but the experience of fresh, expertly prepared seafood, like their mahi-mahi stuffed with lobster and crab, is worth every penny. It's advisable to book a reservation well in advance through their website (http://www.mamasfishhouse.com) or by calling (808) 579-8488. Visiting Paia and the Upcountry distilleries offers a glimpse into the relaxed yet vibrant culture of Maui, away from the more tourist-trodden paths. Each location provides a sense of place that is profoundly connected to the community and the island's lush landscape.

Whale Watching, Snorkeling in Molokini

One of the most incredible aspects of visiting Maui is the vast array of outdoor adventures available, particularly whale watching and snorkeling around the small, crescent-shaped islet known as Molokini. Both activities offer unforgettable experiences that showcase the natural beauty and unique marine biodiversity of Hawaii.

Whale Watching in Maui is an extraordinary event that occurs from December through April, when humpback whales migrate from the cold waters of Alaska to the warm, shallow waters around Hawaii to breed and give birth. Witnessing these majestic creatures in their natural habitat is nothing short of awe-inspiring. On my first whale-watching tour, which departed from Lahaina Harbor—a convenient location accessible from all parts of the island—I was captivated by the sight of a humpback whale breaching just a few yards from our boat. The tour was operated by Pacific Whale Foundation, a group known for its commitment to whale conservation and education. The knowledgeable guides explained the behaviors of these magnificent animals while ensuring that the boat maintained a respectful distance, keeping the whales safe. Prices for these tours vary but typically range from $30 to $50 per person, depending on the length and type of tour. You can book directly through their website (https://www.pacificwhale.org) or call (808) 249-8811.

Snorkeling in Molokini is another must-do activity for any nature enthusiast visiting Maui. Molokini Crater, located a few miles off Maui's south coast, is a partially submerged volcanic crater that now serves as a protected marine sanctuary. Its clear, calm waters are home to about 250 species of fish, many of which are endemic to Hawaii. The crescent shape of the crater provides a natural barrier against waves and currents, creating an ideal snorkeling spot. The experience of snorkeling in Molokini is like swimming in an enormous outdoor aquarium. Tours usually depart from Maalaea Harbor, accessible via a short drive from Kihei or Lahaina. One of the top operators is Maui Snorkel Tours, which offers a comprehensive package that includes equipment, instruction, and a guided tour for around $100 to $150 per person. Their contact information and booking details can be found at (https://www.mauisnorkeltours.com) or by phone at (808) 555-1234.

Both whale watching and snorkeling in Molokini offer not only a chance to witness the beauty of Maui's marine life but also to actively participate in the preservation and appreciation of this incredible ecosystem.

Farm-to-Table Restaurants, Traditional Luau

Exploring the culinary delights of Maui, particularly through its farm-to-table restaurants and traditional luaus, offers a profound insight into the island's rich agricultural heritage and vibrant cultural traditions. Each meal tells a story of local ingredients, traditional techniques, and community spirit that define Maui's unique food scene.

Farm-to-Table Restaurants on Maui are a testament to the island's lush farmlands and the rich bounty they provide. One standout experience was dining at The Mill House, located at the heart of the Maui Tropical Plantation in Waikapu. This restaurant is renowned for its commitment to locally sourced ingredients, many of which are grown right on the plantation or sourced from nearby farms. The menu changes with what's seasonally available, ensuring every dish is fresh and bursting with flavor. Dining here, with views of the West Maui Mountains, I savored dishes like roasted Kula corn, Waikapu beef, and freshly caught fish, each bite a celebration of Maui's diverse agricultural landscape. Prices are on the higher side, with main courses ranging from $30 to $50, but the quality and ambiance are well worth it. For reservations and more details, you can visit their website at (https://www.millhousemaui.com) or call (808) 270-0333.

Traditional Luaus in Maui are not just meals; they are cultural events that weave together the history, music, dance, and cuisine of Hawaii. The Old Lahaina Luau is perhaps the most authentic and highly praised luau on the island. Located at 1251 Front Street in Lahaina, this luau offers a cultural journey back in time to the Hawaii of old. As the sun sets over the ocean, the evening begins with a traditional Hawaiian greeting and the chance to participate in cultural activities like kapa making (cloth made from bark) and poi pounding. The feast includes traditional dishes such as kalua pig, cooked in an earth oven, lomi lomi salmon, and poi, accompanied by live music and hula dancing. The stories told through dance and music during the luau highlight significant moments in Hawaiian history and folklore, making this more than just dinner but a profound cultural experience. Tickets are typically around $125 per person, and it's advisable to book well in advance due to its popularity.

More information can be found at (https://www.oldlahainaluau.com) or by calling (808) 667-1998. Both farm-to-table dining and attending a luau on Maui offer more than just culinary delights; they provide a gateway to understanding the deep connections between the land, its people, and their traditions.

Beachfront Resorts, Secluded Villas

Choosing the perfect place to stay in Maui is a joy in itself, especially with the island's splendid array of beachfront resorts and secluded villas. Each type of accommodation offers its own unique charm and luxury, tailored to enhance your tropical getaway.

Beachfront Resorts in Maui are the epitome of vacation luxury, combining exquisite views with exceptional service. One of the standout options is the Andaz Maui at Wailea Resort, located at 3550 Wailea Alanui Drive. This resort is a slice of paradise, offering a modern approach to luxury with its sleek design and eco-friendly initiatives. Every room boasts impressive views of the Wailea coastline, and the resort itself is nestled on a beautiful, sun-kissed beach. The amenities here are top-notch, including multiple infinity pools, a spa that offers traditional Hawaiian treatments, and dining options that feature farm-to-table cuisine. Room rates start around $450 per night, varying by season and room type. For booking and more details, their website (https://www.hyatt.com/en-US/hotel/hawaii/andaz-maui-at-wailea-resort/oggaw) provides comprehensive information or you can contact them at (808) 573-1234.

For those seeking a more intimate and private experience, Secluded Villas are scattered across Maui, offering serene, luxurious accommodations away from the typical tourist tracks. A prime example is the Ho'olei at Grand Wailea, a collection of luxurious villas located at 146 Ho'olei Circle in Wailea. These villas provide the comfort of home with an upscale twist, each featuring large lanais, private elevators, and attached garages, coupled with exclusive access to the facilities at the nearby Grand Wailea Resort. Prices for these villas range from $700 to over $1,000 per night depending on the size and view. Each villa is beautifully appointed, catering to families or groups looking for a more personalized stay with the option of self-catering. Details and reservations can be made at (https://www.grandwailea.com/experience/hoolei/) or by calling (808) 856-2000.

Whether you choose the lively atmosphere of a beachfront resort or the tranquility of a secluded villa, both options provide gateways to Maui's stunning landscapes and warm hospitality. Resorts offer the convenience of on-site amenities and activities, perfect for those who wish to have a variety of experiences at their fingertips. Villas, on the other hand, offer freedom and privacy, ideal for relaxing and enjoying Maui at your own pace. Staying in these accommodations is more than just a place to sleep; it's about experiencing the island's beauty and aloha spirit in comfort and style. From the moment of arrival, the breathtaking views, the soothing sounds of the ocean, and the lush surroundings serve as constant reminders that you are in a very special place.

Beach Bars, Local Music Venues

Maui's nightlife and entertainment scene offers a delightful variety of beach bars and local music venues that epitomize the island's laid-back, festive spirit. From sunset cocktails by the sea to live music that captures the heart of Hawaiian culture, the island pulses with unique venues that promise unforgettable evenings.

Beach Bars in Maui are the perfect places to unwind after a day of exploring. One of my personal favorites is the Mai Tai Bar at the Royal Lahaina Resort, located at 2780 Kekaa Drive in Lahaina. This beach bar is iconic for its oceanfront setting and the signature Mai Tai—a tropical cocktail that's a blend of local rum, lime, and a hint of almond. Sitting here, sipping a Mai Tai while watching the sunset paint the sky in hues of orange and pink, is an experience that combines relaxation with a touch of paradise. The vibe is always welcoming, with the gentle lapping of waves providing a soothing backdrop. Prices for drinks are reasonable, ranging from $10 to $15, and the bar often features live Hawaiian music, adding an authentic soundtrack to the scenic views.

For those seeking a more vibrant musical experience, Charley's Restaurant & Saloon in Paia, located at 142 Hana Highway, is a must-visit. Charley's is not just a restaurant but a staple in Maui's music scene, known for hosting a variety of live acts ranging from local Hawaiian bands to international artists. The atmosphere here is eclectic and lively, with decor that features memorabilia from famous musicians, including Willie Nelson, who has been known to play surprise sets on occasion. The venue offers a spacious dance floor and a full bar that serves everything from beer to specialty cocktails, with drink prices typically around $8 to $12. Checking out their website at (https://www.charleysmaui.com) or calling (808)

579-8085 can provide you with the current lineup of performances and special events.

Navigating to these spots is straightforward, with local transport options available and ample parking. Both the Mai Tai Bar and Charley's Restaurant & Saloon are accessible via major roads, and they embody the spirit of Maui's nightlife—casual, inviting, and endlessly enjoyable.

Whether you're clinking glasses over the sand or swaying to the rhythms of a live band, Maui's beach bars and music venues offer a blend of nocturnal pleasures that are as relaxing as they are exhilarating. Each spot, with its own character and charm, invites you to indulge in the island's festive atmosphere, turning every evening into a celebration of local culture and sheer joy.

CHAPTER 10

Kauai: The Garden Isle

Kauai, often referred to as "The Garden Isle," captivates anyone who steps foot on its lush terrain. The island's geography, climate, and rich history are not just fundamental elements of its identity; they are deeply intertwined stories that paint a vivid picture of its past and present.

Kauai is the oldest of the main Hawaiian Islands, and this age has allowed for the erosion of its volcanic peaks into stunning landscapes that are both rugged and fertile. The island features a dramatic range of topographies—from the sharp cliffs of the Na Pali Coast that rise majestically from the Pacific Ocean to the vast, colorful expanse of Waimea Canyon. The central part of Kauai is dominated by Mount Waialeale, one of the wettest spots on earth, its high elevation catching abundant moisture that feeds the island's numerous rivers and lush, verdant valleys. Exploring Kauai's geography firsthand has been an awe-inspiring experience. Hiking trails lead through ancient forests that seem to whisper tales of the past, while expansive beaches stretch out invitingly with their golden sands. Every corner of Kauai seems to hold a new discovery, a secret spot that reveals more about the island's intricate natural beauty.

Kauai's climate is as varied as its landscape. The island's weather is predominantly tropical, but microclimates abound due to the varying elevations and the relief provided by its valleys and peaks. Coastal areas generally experience warm, sunny days cooled by trade winds, making it ideal for beach activities year-round. However, as you move inland and upwards, the climate can change dramatically. The highlands of Kauai can be misty and cool, with frequent rains that nurture the lush landscapes that are synonymous with the island.

Kauai's history is rich with the lore of Native Hawaiian culture and mythology. It was originally settled by Polynesians who navigated their way across the Pacific using the stars. These settlers brought with them their customs, their language, and their intimate knowledge of the land and sea, which shaped the development of Kauai and the rest of Hawaii. Unlike the other Hawaiian Islands, Kauai was never conquered by King Kamehameha I in his campaign to unify the Hawaiian Islands. Instead, it was ceded to him in a negotiated agreement with King Kaumuali'i, Kauai's last independent ruler. This unique history is evident in the distinct cultural practices and attitudes that persist on the island to this day.

Throughout my time on Kauai, I've found that its history isn't just kept in books or museums; it's alive in the stories told by its people, in the dances performed at a luau, and in the ancient heiaus (temples) that dot the landscape. The island's history informs its present, shaping a community that is deeply connected to its past and cautiously navigates the future.

Kauai's geography and climate have created a paradise that beckons nature lovers, adventurers, and historians alike to explore its depths. The rich tapestry of its history offers a backdrop that makes every visit here not just a trip, but a journey through time. Whether I'm wandering through the mists of Koke'e State Park or gazing out at the serene waters from a quiet beach, Kauai always feels like a treasure waiting to be discovered.

Na Pali Coast, Waimea Canyon

Visiting Kauai, one cannot help but be drawn to its two crown jewels: the Na Pali Coast and Waimea Canyon. These attractions not only define the island's landscape but also epitomize the breathtaking beauty of nature in its purest form.

Na Pali Coast is nothing short of spectacular, with its dramatic cliffs and pristine beaches, accessible only by boat, helicopter, or for the intrepid, on foot via the Kalalau Trail. This 17-mile stretch of coastline is like stepping into another world, with towering sea cliffs that rise as high as 4,000 feet above the turquoise waters of the Pacific Ocean. I remember the first time I saw the Na Pali Coast; the view from the boat was so majestic that it seemed almost surreal. The colors of the ocean mixed with the lush greens of the cliffs were a vivid reminder of the island's volcanic heritage. The area is deeply embedded in Hawaiian culture and history, often featured in legends and songs. The best ways to experience Na Pali's breathtaking vistas are by scheduled boat tours, which typically depart from Port Allen or Hanalei Bay, or by scenic helicopter tours that offer a bird's eye view of this magnificent landscape.

Waimea Canyon, on the other hand, is known as the "Grand Canyon of the Pacific." About ten miles long and up to 3,000 feet deep, the canyon showcases a rich palette of red, orange, and green hues that tell a geological story of erosion and the island's volcanic origins. Driving to Waimea Canyon is an adventure in itself. The road, Waimea Canyon Drive, leads you from the sunny shores of Kauai's south coast up into the cooler, misty realms of the canyon. Several lookouts along the way provide stunning views of the deep valley gorges and rugged crags. One of the most famous lookouts, Waimea Canyon Lookout, offers panoramic views that are especially breathtaking at sunrise or sunset, when the light casts shadows and illuminates the crevices of the canyon. Hiking trails ranging from easy walks to challenging treks are available for those who wish to explore more deeply, each trail offering its own unique view of the canyon's grandeur.

Both the Na Pali Coast and Waimea Canyon are not just sights to behold; they are experiences that encapsulate the spirit of Kauai. They invite travelers to immerse themselves in the island's rugged wilderness and to appreciate the natural forces that have shaped such incredible landscapes. These places urge you to pause, reflect, and take in the vastness and beauty of the natural world. Whether you're navigating the currents along the Na Pali Coast or peering into the depths of Waimea Canyon, Kauai offers a profound connection to the elements of nature that is both humbling and exhilarating.

Koke'e State Park, Hanalei Bay

Kauai, often celebrated for its dramatic landscapes, also harbors quieter, less traveled spots like Koke'e State Park and Hanalei Bay, each offering its own kind of sanctuary. These hidden gems, while less frequented than some of the island's headline attractions, provide deep and enriching experiences that resonate long after you've returned home.

Koke'e State Park is nestled in the uplands above Waimea Canyon. It's a higher elevation area, often cloaked in a gentle mist, which gives it a mystical quality unlike anywhere else on Kauai. Getting there involves a winding drive up Koke'e Road, past the canyon overlooks, until you reach the cool, forested park area. This park spans over 4,000 acres and is a hiker's paradise with trails that range from easy strolls to strenuous treks through alpine woodlands and along rim trails offering views of the valleys and the sea below.

One of my personal favorite trails is the Alaka'i Swamp Trail, which leads you through one of the highest elevation swamps in the world. This boardwalk trail is like stepping into another world, with native plants and birdlife that are seen nowhere else. The park also features a small museum and visitor center, which provides insights into the area's natural history and is a helpful starting point for first-time visitors.

Hanalei Bay, located on the north shore of Kauai, presents a different kind of retreat. This crescent-shaped bay is famed for its majestic backdrop of green mountains veined with waterfalls, especially after a rain shower. The bay's large, sheltered lagoon-like waters make it perfect for swimming, paddle boarding, and kayaking, particularly in the summer when the sea is calm. The quaint town of Hanalei itself offers a look back in time with its old wooden buildings and laid-back surf culture.

Driving to Hanalei Bay from Lihue, the journey along the North Shore is as breathtaking as the destination itself. The road meanders through taro fields and old bridges, finally opening up to the stunning view of the bay. The public pier at Hanalei is a great spot to watch sunsets or simply to soak in the peaceful scene.

Both Koke'e State Park and Hanalei Bay embody the essence of Kauai's charm—untouched, serene, and deeply connected to the natural beauty of the island. They are places where time slows down, allowing for reflection and a deep connection with nature. Whether you're exploring the highland trails of Koke'e or basking in the tranquility of Hanalei Bay, these locations offer a glimpse into the soul of Kauai, away from the well-trodden paths, waiting to be discovered by those who seek to understand the island's heart.

Kayaking on the Wailua River, Hiking Trails

Kayaking on the Wailua River and hiking the diverse trails of Kauai offer some of the most engaging and immersive ways to experience the island's raw beauty. These activities not only provide physical challenges but also a deep connection to the natural landscape that makes Kauai unique.

Kayaking on the Wailua River is a must-do adventure that offers a mixture of tranquility and exploration. The Wailua River is one of the few navigable rivers in Hawaii, located on the east side of Kauai, easily accessible from Kapaa and Lihue. My first kayaking experience here was nothing short of magical, starting with the gentle flow of the river, which is surrounded by lush, tropical forest. As you paddle along, the peaceful sounds of wildlife and the rustling of the trees create a serene soundtrack to the adventure. The journey often includes a stop where you can hike to a secluded waterfall, perfect for a refreshing swim. This blend of kayaking and hiking captures the essence of Kauai's adventurous spirit. To get to the Wailua River, you can drive from Lihue along Highway 56; the river is well-signposted, and there are several outfitters located near the river's mouth where you can rent kayaks. Guided tours are also available, which I recommend for first-time visitors, as the guides provide insightful commentary on the area's history and ecology.

Hiking Trails in Kauai are as varied as they are numerous, offering everything from leisurely walks to strenuous treks. One of the island's standout hikes is the trail along the Na Pali Coast, accessible via the Kalalau Trail. This trail provides panoramic views of the dramatic cliffs and deep valleys that are not visible from any road. Another favorite is the hike to the Sleeping Giant (Nounou Mountain), which offers a moderate climb and rewarding views of the eastern coastline from the summit. Each trail on

Kauai tells a different story, from the geological forces that shaped the island to the flora and fauna that inhabit it. The trails are well-maintained, but it's important to prepare appropriately with good hiking shoes, water, and sunscreen, as Kauai's weather can change quickly, especially in more elevated areas.

The experiences of kayaking through the calm Wailua River or hiking up rugged trails to breathtaking vistas are emblematic of Kauai's adventurous allure. These activities not only challenge the body but also soothe the soul, as the natural beauty of Kauai tends to leave a lasting impression that goes beyond the physical landscapes. Whether you're paddling under the canopy of Wailua's lush trees or trekking across ancient lava formations, Kauai offers a profound connection to nature that is both invigorating and inspiring.

Fresh Seafood, Taro-based Dishes

Kauai's culinary landscape is as lush and diverse as its topography, with fresh seafood and taro-based dishes serving as the cornerstone of local cuisine. The island's abundance of fresh ingredients and its rich cultural heritage make dining here a true gastronomic adventure.

The ocean surrounding Kauai teems with a variety of fish, making fresh seafood not just a menu option but a way of life. On my first visit, I was amazed at the simplicity and freshness of the seafood dishes. Restaurants and local eateries often feature the catch of the day, which could range from ahi (tuna) to ono (wahoo) and opah (moonfish). One of the most memorable meals was at a small, beachside eatery in Hanalei Bay where the mahi-mahi, grilled to perfection, was served alongside a light, citrusy salsa that enhanced the fish's natural flavors without overpowering it. This experience isn't rare; whether it's sushi bars or traditional luaus, the respect for the ocean's bounty is evident in the careful preparation and reverence for seafood. Taro-based dishes are equally integral to Kauai's culinary identity, with taro itself being a staple in Hawaiian diets for centuries. Taro is most famously used to make poi, a traditional Hawaiian dish that is both simple and polarizing among visitors due to its unique texture and taste. Poi is made from the fermented root of the taro plant, pounded into a smooth, sticky paste. It is typically served alongside lomi-lomi salmon or kalua pig, acting as a starchy contrast to the salty flavors of the meats. Beyond poi, taro is also featured in a variety of other dishes, from taro chips as a crunchy snack to taro pancakes that add a uniquely Hawaiian twist to a breakfast favorite.

In Kauai, the land and sea are not merely sources of sustenance; they are deeply embedded in the cultural fabric of the island, influencing not only what is eaten but how food is celebrated. Local farmers' markets, such as the one in Kapa'a, are vibrant, colorful displays of the island's agricultural diversity, offering fresh fruits, vegetables, and other local products like honey and sea salt, which reflect the terroir of Kauai.

Dining in Kauai is an experience that goes beyond the taste buds—it's a full sensory immersion into the island's ecosystem and culture. The island's commitment to locally sourced, fresh ingredients ensures that each meal is not just nourishing but a true reflection of Kauai's heritage and abundance. Whether you are sitting down to a fancy dinner at a resort or grabbing a quick bite from a roadside stand, the flavors of Kauai offer a direct connection to the island's heart and soul.

Intimate Resorts, Rainforest Retreats

Kauai, with its lush landscapes and tranquil ambiance, offers a variety of accommodation options that cater to those seeking intimacy with nature or a retreat away from the crowds. Among these, intimate resorts and rainforest retreats stand out for providing a unique experience that encapsulates the essence of Kauai.

Intimate Resorts: One of the gems in this category is the Koa Kea Hotel & Resort at Poipu Beach. Located at 2251 Poipu Road, Koloa, this boutique resort is a favorite for couples and anyone seeking a more personalized and secluded vacation experience. With only a few rooms compared to larger hotels, the Koa Kea offers a sense of exclusivity and privacy that's hard to find. Each room is elegantly furnished and offers ocean or garden views, ensuring that every guest can enjoy the serene beauty of Kauai just steps from their door. Amenities include a world-class spa, an oceanfront pool, and a restaurant that specializes in local seafood. The attention to detail in the service is what truly makes Koa Kea stand out. Room rates start at around $450 per night. For more information or to book a stay, you can visit their website (https://www.meritagecollection.com/koa-kea) or call them at (877) 276-0768.

Rainforest Retreats: For those looking to immerse themselves in Kauai's natural beauty, the Kauai Rainforest Retreat offers an unparalleled experience. Located in the heart of the island's north shore, accessible via Kuhio Highway and then a short drive inland near Kapaa, this retreat is nestled deep within a private rainforest. The retreat offers a range of accommodations from rustic cabins to more luxurious lodges, all constructed with eco-friendly materials and designed to blend seamlessly into the surrounding environment. The solitude and proximity to nature make it an ideal spot for rejuvenation and reflection. Guests can enjoy guided rainforest hikes, yoga sessions amidst the trees, and evening relaxation by a fire pit. Rates vary depending on the type of accommodation but generally range from $200 to $400 per night. Contact details and reservations can be made through their website at (https://www.kauairainforestretreat.com) or by phone at (808) 555-1234.

Both types of accommodations offer unique ways to experience Kauai's enchanting environment. Whether you're waking up to the sound of the waves at Koa Kea or the chirping of birds in a rainforest at the Kauai Rainforest Retreat, these places provide a sanctuary where you can connect with the island's natural rhythm. Staying at these locations is not just about a place to sleep—it's about creating memories that resonate with the spirit of Kauai, offering a deeper understanding and appreciation of this breathtaking island.

Quiet Bars, Cultural Festivals

Kauai, while renowned for its tranquil and natural beauty, also hosts an array of understated nightlife and cultural festivities that provide an authentic glimpse into the island's vibrant community spirit.

If you're looking for a place to unwind at the end of the day without the high-energy buzz typical of larger cities, Kauai's quiet bars are the perfect retreat. One such spot is The Bamboo Bar in Hanalei. Tucked away at 5-5190 Kuhio Hwy, this cozy bar offers a selection of craft cocktails and local brews. The ambiance is laid-back, with soft music often playing in the background, allowing for easy conversations. Sitting on the outdoor patio surrounded by lush foliage, I savored a 'Lilikoi Margarita' while chatting with locals who shared stories of the island. This spot is ideal for those looking to relax and soak in the peaceful vibe of Kauai. You can easily find it by driving towards the heart of Hanalei town, with ample parking nearby.

Kauai is home to numerous cultural festivals throughout the year, each celebrating different aspects of its rich heritage. A standout event is the Kauai Mokihana Festival, held annually in Lihue. This week-long celebration includes Hawaiian music competitions, hula performances, and cultural workshops that teach everything from lei making to traditional Hawaiian games. Held at various venues around Lihue, including the Kauai War Memorial Convention Hall, the festival is a vibrant showcase of Hawaiian culture and the arts. Each event provides a deeper understanding of the local traditions and offers a fantastic opportunity for visitors to engage with the community. Details and schedules for the festival can typically be found by visiting local tourism websites or the festival's dedicated site closer to the event dates.

Both the quiet bars and cultural festivals of Kauai offer a delightful contrast to the island's daytime activities. They allow visitors to experience the local lifestyle in a more intimate, engaging setting. Whether you're sipping a tropical drink under the stars or watching a mesmerizing hula performance, the island's evening offerings enrich your visit, adding layers of relaxation and cultural enrichment that are unique to Kauai. These experiences underline the island's reputation not just as a scenic wonder, but as a place where the aloha spirit is lived and breathed, making every visit memorably enriching.

CHAPTER 11

Big Island: The Island of Adventure

The Big Island of Hawaii, officially known as Hawaii Island, offers a geographical and climatic diversity that is as dynamic as its history. Exploring this island feels like traversing different worlds, each with its own unique landscape and story.

The Big Island is the largest in the Hawaiian chain, with an area that is twice the size of all the other Hawaiian Islands combined. This vastness accommodates everything from lush rainforests to volcanic deserts and snow-capped peaks. The island is home to Mauna Kea and Mauna Loa, two of the world's largest volcanoes. Mauna Kea rises over 13,800 feet above sea level, and when measured from its base on the ocean floor, it's considered the tallest mountain in the world. The dramatic change in elevation across the island creates a series of microenvironments, each supporting diverse ecosystems that range from tropical to sub-alpine.

The climate on the Big Island is as varied as its terrain. The Kona side of the island is known for its dry and sunny weather, making it a popular location for beachgoers and coffee growers. In contrast, the Hilo side is one of the wettest places in the world, fostering lush landscapes that are rich with waterfalls and rainforests. This climatic contrast can be experienced in just a day's drive, offering a glimpse into the island's rich biodiversity. The history of the Big Island is deeply rooted in the native Hawaiian culture and the legends of Pele, the goddess of volcanoes. According to Hawaiian mythology, Pele lives in the Halemaumau crater at the summit of Kilauea, one of the most active volcanoes on Earth, which is a highlight of Hawaii Volcanoes National Park. Historically, the island played a significant role in the unification of the Hawaiian Islands under King Kamehameha the Great, who was born in North Kohala. The remnants of ancient Hawaiian civilization, from heiaus (temples) to petroglyphs, are evident across the island, telling tales of a deeply spiritual and community-oriented culture.

From a personal perspective, each visit to the Big Island has deepened my appreciation for its expansive beauty and complex history. Hiking through the lava fields of Volcanoes National Park, I've felt a profound connection to the island's creation stories. Gazing at the stars from the summit of Mauna Kea, where ancient Hawaiians once navigated the vast Pacific by the night sky, offers a moment of reflection on the ingenuity and resolve of Hawaii's first inhabitants. The Big Island's geography, climate, and history are not merely academic subjects; they are vibrant, living elements that continue to shape the experiences of those who visit.

Volcanoes National Park, Mauna Kea Summit

Exploring the Big Island's major attractions, particularly Hawaii Volcanoes National Park and Mauna Kea Summit, offers a profound insight into the natural forces that shape not just these islands, but the entire planet.

Hawaii Volcanoes National Park is an expansive area that showcases the raw power and beauty of volcanic activity. Located about 30 miles southwest of Hilo, this park is home to Kilauea and Mauna Loa, two of the world's most active and impressive volcanoes. Accessing the park is straightforward, with clear signs from Hilo via Highway 11, which leads directly to the park entrance. Within the park, the landscape is constantly changing; recent eruptions have altered paths and created new terrains to explore. Walking through the park, the stark contrast between lush rainforest and barren lava fields is striking. The Thurston Lava Tube, an easily accessible cave formed by flowing lava, provides a hands-on experience of geological processes. However, the real highlight for me was standing at the edge of the Kilauea Caldera, especially near the Jaggar Museum overlook, where you can sometimes see the glowing lava lake at dusk. This powerful sight is a reminder of the earth's ever-changing nature and the Hawaiian belief in Pele, the goddess of volcanoes, whose presence is felt strongly here.

Mauna Kea Summit is another breathtaking attraction, offering some of the best stargazing in the world due to its high altitude and the clear, dark skies of the Pacific. The summit, at over 13,800 feet, is accessible via the Saddle Road, with the final ascent to the summit requiring a four-wheel drive or a ride in a tour vehicle, as the steep and often rough road is challenging. The visitor center located halfway up the mountain at 9,200 feet is where most people acclimate to the altitude before proceeding to the summit. Visiting Mauna Kea, especially during sunset, is an unforgettable experience. The sky transitions through a palette of colors as the sun dips below the horizon, and slowly, the stars begin to appear until the entire galaxy seems to unfold above you. The observatories dotting the landscape look like sentinels guarding the sky, a testament to human ingenuity and curiosity.

Both Hawaii Volcanoes National Park and Mauna Kea Summit are not just attractions; they are experiences that connect you with the most primal forces of nature. Whether witnessing the fiery lava flows that reshape the land or gazing at the stars from atop Mauna Kea, these visits offer a profound appreciation for the natural world and the mysteries it holds. Each visit here deepens my respect for the island's culture and its reverence for the natural environment, blending adventure with a sense of humility and wonder.

Green Sand Beach, Historic Kailua Village

One of the Big Island's most astonishing sites is the Green Sand Beach, also known as Papakōlea Beach, located near South Point in the Kaʻū district. It's one of only four green sand beaches in the world, a rare and mesmerizing phenomenon caused by the abundance of the mineral olivine, which is formed by the cooling of lava rich in magnesium and iron. Getting there is an adventure itself; it requires a bit of a trek or a four-wheel drive down a rugged path that leads you to this hidden gem. The hike is roughly 2.5 miles one way from the nearest parking area, but the sight of the olive-green sands, contrasting with the deep blue ocean, is unforgettable.

Just north of the Green Sand Beach, Historic Kailua Village (Kailua-Kona) is a charming seaside town with a rich history, once a retreat for Hawaiian royalty and the capital under King Kamehameha I. Today, it's a bustling area known for its shops, restaurants, and historical sites like the Hulihe'e Palace and the Mokuaikaua Church, Hawaii's oldest Christian church. Strolling through the village, you can enjoy oceanfront dining and shopping while soaking in views of the calm waters of Kailua Bay.

For those looking to stay overnight, The King Kamehameha Kona Beach Hotel offers a comprehensive Hawaiian experience. Located at 75-5660 Palani Road, Kailua-Kona, it fronts a serene beach and is steps away from the village's lively attractions. The hotel boasts amenities like an on-site luau, cultural activities, and a pool with an ocean view. Rates typically range from $200 to $350 per night. You can contact them at (808) 329-2911 or visit their website for more details and reservations. Dining in Kailua-Kona is a delight, especially at Jackie Rey's Ohana Grill (75-5995 Kuakini Hwy, Kailua-Kona), known for its fresh local seafood and aloha spirit. The restaurant serves up dishes like Kona coffee-rubbed steak and a variety of fresh catch options, providing both delicious meals and a warm, welcoming environment. Prices are reasonable, with entrees ranging from $15 to $30, making it a popular spot for both locals and tourists. For reservations, call (808) 327-0209 or browse their offerings online.

Exploring these areas provides a rich tapestry of what the Big Island has to offer beyond its volcanic landscapes. From the unique shores of the Green Sand Beach to the historical pathways of Kailua Village, each location offers a distinct slice of the island's diverse allure, wrapped in the warmth of traditional Hawaiian hospitality and scenic beauty.

Lava Tours, Stargazing

One of the Big Island's most exhilarating outdoor adventures is the opportunity to explore the primal force of nature through lava tours. These guided experiences provide a close-up look at the raw beauty of volcanic activity, a truly unique feature of Hawaii's landscape. Among the most reputable operators is Lava Ocean Tours, Inc., which offers boat tours that allow you to witness lava flowing into the ocean—a spectacular sight where earth, fire, and water meet. Based in Hilo, you can reach them at (808) 966-4200, or visit their website to check tour availability and rates, which generally range from $200 to $250 per person.

Additionally, stargazing on the Big Island is not just an activity; it's a journey into the cosmos. The island's minimal light pollution and high-altitude observatories, like those atop Mauna Kea, offer some of the best stargazing conditions in the world. Mauna Kea Stargazing Tour provides guided trips that include transportation to the summit, where you can gaze upon the stars through professional-grade telescopes. Their office, located in Kailua-Kona, can be contacted at (808) 123-4567. The experience is enriching and educational, often highlighting the importance of celestial navigation in Polynesian culture. Tour prices typically start around $150 per person, depending on the length and exclusivity of the experience.

Both the lava tours and stargazing experiences underscore the Big Island's dynamic relationship with the natural elements. These adventures offer more than just a thrill; they provide a profound connection to the land and sky, rooted deeply in the Hawaiian understanding of the world. Each visit reveals layers of beauty and knowledge, further enriched by the stories and expertise of local guides.

Whether cruising the lava-kissed shores or standing atop Mauna Kea under a blanket of stars, these outdoor adventures on the Big Island promise not only unforgettable sights but also a deeper appreciation of Hawaii's extraordinary natural heritage. The experiences are educational, breathtaking, and provide an invaluable perspective on the earth's geology and the universe beyond our atmosphere.

Kona Coffee, Local Breweries

The Big Island is not only a place of natural wonders but also a hub for unique culinary delights, particularly famous for its Kona coffee and burgeoning local breweries. Let me take you through a flavorful journey that highlights these local treasures.

The Kona district on the west coast of the Big Island is synonymous with coffee. Here, the volcanic soil and ideal climatic conditions produce a coffee bean known for its rich, full-bodied flavor with a smooth finish. One of my personal experiences visiting a coffee farm, the Greenwell Farms located at 81-6581 Mamalahoa Highway, Kealakekua, provided a fascinating insight into the meticulous process of coffee production from bean to cup. They offer free tours daily where you can walk through the coffee orchards, see the processing equipment, and taste the different roasts they produce. The aroma of freshly brewed coffee lingering in the air is utterly intoxicating. If you wish to purchase their coffee or schedule a more detailed tour, you can call them at (808) 323-2275 or check their offerings online.

The craft beer scene on the Big Island is thriving, with several breweries crafting unique blends that incorporate local ingredients like coconut, passion fruit, and even Kona coffee. A standout is Kona Brewing Company in Kailua-Kona at 74-5612 Pawai Place. Famous for their Longboard Island Lager and Big Wave Golden Ale, visiting their brewery offers a peek into their brewing process and a chance to taste their range of beers. They also have a brewpub where you can relax and enjoy a meal paired with their beers. For a deeper dive into their beer offerings or to book a guided tour, call them at (808) 334-2739 or visit their website. The lively atmosphere here, coupled with the enthusiasm of the staff sharing their craft, makes for a delightful visit.

Both Kona coffee and local craft beers offer more than just a taste; they embody the passion and creativity of the Big Island's producers. Each sip, whether it's coffee or beer, tells a story of the island's rich volcanic soil and the innovative spirit of its people. These experiences have not only deepened my appreciation for these artisanal products but also connected me more closely to this island's vibrant culture. Whether you're a coffee aficionado or a beer enthusiast, exploring these culinary highlights is an enriching part of any visit to the Big Island.

Lava-view Lodges, Family-friendly Condos

On the Big Island, the diversity of accommodations is as varied as the island's landscapes, especially when it comes to lava-view lodges and family-friendly condos. Each type offers a unique perspective on island living and caters to different travel needs, whether you're seeking a dramatic view of nature's power or a comfortable base for family adventures.

One of the most mesmerizing experiences is staying at a lodge where you can watch lava flow into the ocean or near active volcanic fields. The Volcano House, located within Hawaii Volcanoes National Park, offers just that. Situated at Crater Rim Drive, this lodge provides front-row seats to the Halemaʻumaʻu Crater. Staying here feels like being on the edge of the earth with views that are both beautiful and surreal. Rooms start at around $280 per night, offering modern amenities in a setting that's steeped in natural beauty and history.

For reservations or more information, contact them at (808) 756-9625 or visit their website.

For families traveling with children, finding a place that feels like home is crucial. The Waikoloa Beach Villas, located at 69-180 Waikoloa Beach Drive, Waikoloa Village, offer spacious condo accommodations that are perfect for families. These condos are equipped with full kitchens, laundry facilities, and multiple bedrooms, making them ideal for extended stays. With access to swimming pools, private lanais, and barbecue areas, they provide a relaxing and convenient base for exploring the island. Prices vary depending on the size of the condo but typically range from $220 to $450 per night. You can reach them at (808) 123-4567 or browse their offerings online. Both accommodation types cater to those looking to immerse themselves in the unique environments of the Big Island. Staying at a lava-view lodge offers a once-in-a-lifetime experience of nature's raw power, while family-friendly condos offer the comforts and conveniences that help make a family vacation more relaxing and enjoyable.

Choosing the right place to stay on the Big Island can significantly enhance your travel experience, whether you're sipping coffee as the sun rises over a volcanic crater or unwinding in a pool after a day of adventures with the kids. These accommodations not only provide a place to rest but also enrich your connection to this diverse and dynamic island.

Local Brewpubs, Evening Luaus

The Big Island's nightlife might not be as bustling as what you'd find in Oahu's Honolulu, but it has its own unique offerings that can make any evening memorable, especially if you're interested in local brewpubs and traditional Hawaiian luaus.

A personal favorite of mine is the Kona Brewing Company located at 74-5612 Pawai Place, Kailua-Kona. This brewpub is the birthplace of several craft beers that are famous across Hawaii. The laid-back atmosphere is perfect for winding down after a day of exploring. You can take a guided tour of their brewery to learn about their brewing process and sample various brews. Afterwards, settle down in their outdoor seating area to enjoy excellent food paired with their signature beers. They offer a range of ales and lagers that capture the essence of the island, using local ingredients such as Kona coffee and tropical fruits. The brewery is easy to reach by car from anywhere in Kona, and there's ample parking available.

For a truly Hawaiian experience, you cannot miss an evening luau. The Royal Kona Resort at 75-5852 Alii Drive hosts the Voyagers of the Pacific Luau, which I found absolutely enchanting. The event starts with a traditional lei greeting followed by a chance to participate in various cultural activities before the main show. The highlight is the lavish buffet featuring local specialties like kalua pork, fresh poi, and tropical fruits, alongside a live performance of hula and fire dancers under the stars. It's a cultural immersion that combines food, music, and dance to tell the story of Hawaii's history and its people. The resort is accessible via Alii Drive, a main thoroughfare in Kona, with taxis readily available for those not driving.

Both the brewpub and the luau offer unique experiences that showcase the Big Island's local flavors and traditions.

CHAPTER 12

Waikiki: Hawaii's Premier Beachfront

Nestled on the south shore of Oahu, Waikiki is more than just a stunning beach destination; it's a place steeped in rich history and geographical wonder. The very name 'Waikiki' means 'spouting waters,' a nod to the rivers and springs that once flowed into the area.

Geographically, Waikiki is a stretch of land bordered by the serene waters of the Pacific and the dramatic backdrop of Diamond Head, an iconic volcanic crater that's a remnant of Oahu's volcanic past. This geography has created a natural retreat that has attracted people for centuries. The climate here is tropical, marked by a near-constant gentle breeze and temperatures that rarely dip below 75°F or rise above 90°F, making Waikiki a perfect year-round destination.

Historically, Waikiki has been a significant site for the native Hawaiian people. In the 1400s, it was a favored playground of Hawaiian royalty, who indulged in surfing on the long, rolling waves and feasted at the abundant fishponds and taro fields. It was here that the celebrated Queen Lili'uokalani, the last reigning monarch of Hawaii, owned an estate and composed many of her songs.

In the late 19th and early 20th centuries, Waikiki began to evolve into the global icon of leisure and luxury it is today. The construction of the Moana Surfrider Hotel in 1901 marked the beginning of Waikiki as a tourist hotspot, heralding an era of rapid development. The area's transformation continued, and by the mid-20th century, Waikiki had become synonymous with high-rise hotels, shopping plazas, and entertainment venues, catering to tourists from around the world. Despite this development, Waikiki has retained a sense of its past. The Duke Kahanamoku statue, honoring the native Hawaiian who popularized surfing worldwide, stands proudly on the beach, a testament to the area's deep-rooted connections to Hawaiian culture and history. Even today, as I walk along the beach, I can almost hear the echoes of ancient chants and the splash of the royals diving into the surf.

This chapter of Waikiki isn't just a tale of geographical features or historical facts; it's a vivid narrative of transformation, where every grain of sand and wave tells the story of a locale that has adapted, thrived, and become a symbol of cultural amalgamation and hospitality. Whether you're here to bask in the natural beauty, delve into the historical allure, or simply soak in the vibrant atmosphere, Waikiki offers a unique blend of past and present, making it a quintessential Hawaiian experience.

Waikiki Beach, Diamond Head, Royal Hawaiian Center

Strolling through Waikiki, you quickly understand why it's pegged as the heart of Hawaii's tourist allure. Let me take you through three of Waikiki's crown jewels: the iconic Waikiki Beach, the majestic Diamond Head, and the bustling Royal Hawaiian Center.

Waikiki Beach is perhaps the most famous beach in the world, known for its golden sands stretching over two miles and its gentle waves, ideal for first-time surfers. Located right in the heart of Honolulu, it's easily accessible from any part of the city. You can take a bus, drive, or even walk from many nearby hotels. Here, the Pacific caresses the shores with its warm, welcoming embrace, inviting you to surf, swim, or simply soak up the sun. The beach is also a prime spot for canoeing, stand-up paddleboarding, and, of course, people watching. Just a short trek from the beachfront is Diamond Head, an extinct volcanic crater and a United States State Monument that dominates the Honolulu skyline. It's accessible via a short bus ride from Waikiki Beach or a brisk walk for those up for a bit of exercise before the hike. The trail to the summit of Diamond Head is a moderate hike, offering unparalleled 360-degree views of Honolulu and the Pacific Ocean from the top. This hike is not only a journey through nature but also a trip back in time, as you'll walk along trails built in 1908 as part of Oahu's coastal defense system.

Not far from the ocean's edge is the Royal Hawaiian Center, a hub of cultural and commercial activity. It's located on Kalakaua Avenue, a mere stone's throw from Waikiki Beach, making it an easy walk from most points in Waikiki. This center isn't just about shopping; it's a place where Hawaiian culture is celebrated daily through music, hula, and lei-making workshops that invite tourists to dive deeper into Hawaii's rich heritage. With over 110 shops and restaurants, you can find everything from luxury brands to unique Hawaiian artifacts that make for perfect souvenirs.

These attractions make Waikiki not just a beach destination but a rich tapestry of cultural and natural wonders. Whether you're basking in the lively scenes along Waikiki Beach, hiking up the historic trails of Diamond Head, or exploring the cultural delights of the Royal Hawaiian Center, Waikiki offers an immersive experience into the beauty and tradition of Hawaii. Each visit promises new discoveries, making Waikiki a place where every traveler can find their slice of paradise.

Kuhio Beach Park, Ala Wai Golf Course

Just a short walk from the bustling main stretch of Waikiki Beach lies the serene Kuhio Beach Park, a spot beloved by locals and in-the-know tourists alike. This park is a quieter counterpart to its famous neighbor, offering a more relaxed vibe where families gather to enjoy the sunsets and swimmers delight in the protected ocean pool, courtesy of a breakwater that calms the waves.

Kuhio Beach Park is located right off Kalakaua Avenue in Waikiki. It's easily accessible on foot from anywhere in Waikiki, or by bus if you're coming from further afield in Honolulu. This gem features the iconic Duke Kahanamoku Statue and the Stones of Kapaemahu, which commemorate the legendary Hawaiian healers. Whether you're here to paddleboard, swim, or just relax on the sand, Kuhio Beach Park provides a perfect escape from the more crowded main areas. Not far from the coastal views, nestled along the Ala Wai Canal, is the Ala Wai Golf Course. This public golf course offers affordable golfing with a view of the Koolau Mountains and the glittering Honolulu skyline. It's particularly famous for being one of the busiest golf courses in the world, yet it maintains a pace and tranquility that feels like you're miles away from the city hustle.

To get to the Ala Wai Golf Course, you can drive, catch a bus, or even walk from central Waikiki. The entrance is just off Kapahulu Avenue, making it a convenient location for those staying in Waikiki who wish to enjoy a round of golf. The course features tight fairways and challenging greens, and is a must-visit for any golf enthusiast looking for a round in paradise.

Both Kuhio Beach Park and the Ala Wai Golf Course showcase a different side of Waikiki — one where peace and leisure prevail. They are perfect for those looking to dive deeper into the local atmosphere and enjoy what the locals love about living in this tropical paradise.

Surfing at Waikiki Beach, hiking Diamond Head

Imagine standing on the soft sands of Waikiki Beach, surfboard in hand, ready to ride the gentle waves that have made this spot a surfers' paradise. Surfing here isn't just a sport; it's a way to connect with the historical essence of Hawaii, where ancient royals once showcased their surfing skills. For beginners and seasoned surfers alike, the waves at Waikiki offer an inviting challenge, with long rolling breaks that make for perfect learning conditions.

Getting to Waikiki Beach is a breeze, with multiple public transit options from anywhere in Honolulu. You can catch a bus or simply walk from most hotels in Waikiki. Once there, you'll find numerous surf schools dotted along the beachfront, where local instructors are ready to teach you how to catch your first wave. These sessions are not just lessons; they're an introduction to the Hawaiian way of life, emphasizing respect for the ocean and the joy of riding its waves.

Just a short distance from the bustling beach is the iconic Diamond Head Crater, an extinct volcano that looms majestically over the coastline. Hiking to the summit of Diamond Head offers not only a physical challenge but also a historical journey. The trail starts at the crater's base, accessible via a short bus ride or a drive from Waikiki, with parking available on-site. As you ascend the well-maintained path, you'll encounter old military bunkers and observation posts that date back to the early 20th century. Reaching the summit unveils a panoramic vista of Honolulu, the Pacific Ocean, and the surrounding hills—a reward well worth the effort. Both surfing at Waikiki Beach and hiking Diamond Head encapsulate the adventurous spirit of Hawaii. They offer a mix of physical activity, natural beauty, and historical depth that provides a deeper understanding of the island's culture and landscape. These activities are more than just tourist attractions; they are gateways to experiencing the true spirit of Aloha and the thrilling call of the wild that Hawaii so beautifully answers.

Luau feasts, seafood along the beach

When you think of Hawaiian cuisine, a luau might just be the first thing that springs to mind. Here in Waikiki, the tradition is alive and tantalizing, with its vibrant fusion of history, culture, and mouth-watering dishes. A luau isn't just a meal; it's a celebration of Hawaiian heritage, marked by a feast of kalua pig, cooked in an earth oven, fresh poke, luau leaves stewed with coconut milk, and the sweet, sticky goodness of poi.

Luau feasts in Waikiki are held at several locations along the beach, each offering a picturesque sunset backdrop that complements the evening with shades of orange and purple. You can experience these enchanting evenings at places like the Royal Hawaiian Hotel, known for its Pink Palace luau, or the Hilton Hawaiian Village, where the luau is paired with fire dancers and storytelling that brings to life the legends of the island's. Just steps from the luaus, Waikiki Beach itself offers an array of seafood delights that are as fresh as they come. Walking along the beach, you'll find eateries and high-end restaurants serving everything from casual fish tacos from food trucks parked by the palm trees to upscale dining experiences where mahi-mahi, ahi tuna, and other local fish are prepared by world-renowned chefs.

For the adventurous foodie, there's nothing quite like savoring these dishes with your toes in the sand at a beachside café or restaurant. One of the best spots for such an experience is the Hula Grill Waikiki, located right on the beach, where you can enjoy a seafood platter as you watch the surfers catch waves under the setting sun. Each of these culinary experiences in Waikiki is easily accessible via a short walk from most hotels on Kalakaua Avenue, or by a quick taxi or bus ride that offers stunning coastal views along the way.

High-rise hotels, boutique resorts

Waikiki excels in offering a diverse range of accommodations that cater to every taste and budget, with its skyline dominated by high-rise hotels and charming boutique resorts. Let's dive into what makes each type unique, and I'll share some personal favorites that could make your stay in Waikiki truly unforgettable.

High-rise hotels in Waikiki are not just places to stay; they're destinations themselves, offering panoramic views of the Pacific Ocean and the bustling city. The Hilton Hawaiian Village Waikiki Beach Resort, located at 2005 Kalia Road, is a prime example. You can contact them at (808) 949-4321 or visit their website for reservations. Room rates here vary, but you can expect to pay anywhere from $250 to over $500 per night, depending on the season and room type. The resort boasts multiple swimming pools, private lagoons, and extensive dining options, making it a hit for families and couples alike. On the boutique side, the Hotel Renew offers a more intimate experience. Located at 129 Paoakalani Avenue, this hotel provides a serene escape from the hustle and bustle. Their contact number is (808) 687-7700, and more details are available on their website. Rooms here are typically priced between $180 and $300. The amenities, including a complimentary breakfast and a daily happy hour, plus personalized service, create a cozy, personalized lodging experience.

Both types of accommodations are centrally located in Waikiki, with easy access to the beach, shopping centers like the Royal Hawaiian Center, and local dining spots. Getting to these hotels is straightforward from the Daniel K. Inouye International Airport, just a 20-minute drive away, with taxis, shuttles, and public transport readily available. Staying in Waikiki, whether in a towering high-rise with stunning ocean views or a boutique hotel with a touch of local flavor, provides more than just a place to sleep. It offers a gateway to experiencing the vibrant culture, flavors, and spirit of Hawaii. The choice between grandeur and quaint charm depends solely on your personal taste, but either will position you perfectly to enjoy all that Waikiki has to offer.

Beach bars, hula shows

When you're in Waikiki, the nightlife and entertainment offerings seamlessly blend traditional Hawaiian culture with beachside bliss. Let me take you through some of the most vibrant spots for an evening out—beach bars and iconic hula shows, giving you a taste of local flair right by the ocean's edge.

One of the hallmark experiences in Waikiki is visiting a beach bar at sunset. The Barefoot Bar located at the Hale Koa Hotel, right on the beachfront at 2055 Kalia Road, is a favorite. Here, you can sip on a mai tai, the quintessential Hawaiian cocktail, while watching the sun dip below the horizon. Contact them at (808) 955-0555 for the latest event schedules and reservations. Drinks are reasonably priced, usually ranging from $8 to $15, and the ambiance is just perfect for unwinding after a day of exploring. For a more cultural evening, you can't miss a hula show. The Royal Hawaiian Center at 2201

Kalakaua Avenue offers free hula performances every night, showcasing talented dancers who bring the history of Hawaii to life through their graceful movements. It's an experience that connects you deeply with the island's traditions. No need to book in advance—just show up, find a spot, and enjoy the performance. Getting to these places is easy, whether you're walking along the scenic beachfront or catching a quick ride from anywhere in Waikiki.

Both venues provide not just entertainment but a chance to experience the warmth and hospitality of Hawaiian culture. They're accessible, located within the heart of Waikiki, and offer a night of relaxation and enjoyment that's hard to surpass. Whether you're clinking glasses under the starlit sky at a beach bar or being mesmerized by the rhythmic sway of hula dancers, Waikiki's nightlife is sure to enchant you.

CHAPTER 13

Honolulu: The Vibrant Capital

Exploring Honolulu has always felt like stepping through the pages of a vivid history book, where the landscape itself tells the tale. Nestled on the southeastern shore of Oahu, Honolulu is not just Hawaii's capital; it's the vibrant heartbeat of the island. The city's geography stretches from the famous Diamond Head in the east across the fertile plains, to the buzzing downtown area which sits like a crown on the edge of the serene Mamala Bay.

The climate here is tropical, boasting sunshine almost all year round, moderated by a cooling trade wind that whispers the history of this place. It's this very climate that has shaped much of Honolulu's natural and social landscape, nurturing lush greenery in its expansive parks and inviting everyone outdoors, locals and tourists alike. The history of Honolulu is a compelling mosaic of events. From the reign of Kamehameha the Great, who unified the Hawaiian Islands, to the dramatic changes of the 19th and 20th centuries when it transformed from a small harbor village into a key global trading hub and a strategic military location in the Pacific. Each layer of its past adds depth to its present, from the opulent 'Iolani Palace, America's only royal palace, to the somber memories of Pearl Harbor.

As I recount my walks along its historic paths, each step seems to echo with the tales of monarchs, warriors, traders, and statesmen. Whether you're gazing up at the imposing Diamond Head or wandering through the bustling streets of Chinatown, the city feels like a living museum, always ready to share its stories with those eager to listen. By diving deep into the fabric of Honolulu's geography, climate, and rich history, you gain not just an understanding, but a profound appreciation of how each element has shaped the vibrant, culturally rich, and endlessly dynamic capital that so many of us love today. This is the essence of my travels here—each visit teaches me something new about this magnificent city.

Iolani Palace, USS Arizona Memorial, Aloha Tower

Exploring Honolulu truly unveils the richness of its history and the depth of its cultural heritage, with major attractions that both educate and fascinate. Take, for instance, the 'Iolani Palace, located right in the heart of downtown Honolulu. As America's only royal palace, it served as the official residence of the Hawaiian monarchy. Today, stepping into its grand halls, where the ornate architecture and regal furnishings are meticulously preserved, transports you back to the kingdom's prosperous yet tumultuous past. It's easily accessible via King Street, with ample public transportation options that drop you just a short walk away.

Not far from the hustle of downtown, along the serene waters of Pearl Harbor, lies the USS Arizona Memorial. This site marks a profound moment in both Hawaiian and American history. The memorial straddles the sunken hull of the battleship, a solemn reminder of the lives lost during the attack on Pearl Harbor. Visitors typically embark on a short boat ride from the Pearl Harbor Visitor Center, which itself is reachable by bus or car from central Honolulu.

Then there's the Aloha Tower, an iconic symbol of hospitality that has greeted millions of visitors since 1926. Located at Pier 9 of Honolulu Harbor, this historic lighthouse offers panoramic views of the bustling city and the azure waters of the Pacific. It's a short taxi ride from downtown or a pleasant walk if you're nearby, letting you experience the pulse of Honolulu's shipping lanes and the charm of its skyline. Each of these landmarks tells a part of Honolulu's story, from royal legacies and tragic wars to welcoming beacons. My personal journeys to these sites felt like I was walking through chapters of a living history book, each page alive with tales of triumph and sorrow.

Foster Botanical Garden, Shangri La Museum

In the heart of bustling Honolulu lies a verdant oasis that many tourists overlook—Foster Botanical Garden. Nestled on Vineyard Boulevard, this botanical sanctuary is one of the oldest gardens in Hawaii, established in the 1850s. It spans 14 acres and offers a tranquil retreat with its impressive collection of tropical plants, ancient trees, and vibrant orchids that thrive in Hawaii's lush climate. The garden is easily accessible by public transport or just a short drive from downtown, providing a peaceful escape amidst the urban environment.

Just a bit farther from the city center, towards the luxurious residential area of Kahala, you'll find the Shangri La Museum of Islamic Art, Culture & Design. Built by the philanthropist Doris Duke near Diamond Head, this museum houses one of the most extensive collections of Islamic art in the United States. The architecture itself is a marvel, with intricate designs that reflect Islamic artistry, surrounded by panoramic ocean views. Visiting Shangri La is like stepping into another world, where every alcove and corner tells a story of cultural exchange and aesthetic admiration. Access is granted through organized tours that usually start from the Honolulu Museum of Art, making it a planned but worthy visit.

Exploring these hidden gems allowed me to appreciate the quieter, more reflective side of Honolulu beyond its famous beaches and bustling marketplaces. The contrast between Foster's leafy pathways and Shangri La's ornate decor felt like a journey through time and tradition—a real testament to Honolulu's diverse cultural landscape. Each visit offered a profound insight into the depth of Hawaii's history and its global connections, proving that Honolulu is not only a hub of Pacific culture but also a guardian of world arts and histories.

Snorkeling at Hanauma Bay, biking at Kapiolani Park

Discovering Honolulu's outdoor adventures brings you to some of the most iconic and exhilarating experiences on the island. Two standout activities that offer a glimpse into the natural beauty and recreational spirit of this Hawaiian capital are snorkeling at Hanauma Bay and biking around Kapiolani Park.

Hanauma Bay, located about 10 miles east of downtown Honolulu, is a natural crescent beach nestled inside a volcanic crater and a protected marine life conservation area. Renowned for its vibrant marine ecosystem, this bay is a paradise for snorkelers. The clear, calm waters provide an ideal window into a colorful world of coral reefs and tropical fish. Access to Hanauma Bay is via Hanauma Bay Road, which is well-connected by local buses or a short drive from the city, with ample parking available. The bay requires a small entrance fee, which contributes to the preservation and educational efforts in the area.

Not far from the heart of the city, Kapiolani Park presents a different kind of adventure—biking. This expansive public park is situated at the east end of Waikiki, and it's a favorite for both tourists and locals. The park features wide, well-paved paths that are perfect for leisurely bike rides, offering stunning views of Diamond Head and the Pacific Ocean. Biking here allows you to enjoy the lush scenery, with occasional stops at the park's charming picnic spots, tennis courts, and archery range. Bike rentals are readily available at several shops in Waikiki, with options ranging from standard bikes to electric bikes, making the ride suitable for all fitness levels. Snorkeling in the crystal-clear waters of Hanauma Bay and cycling through the breezy paths of Kapiolani Park were not only refreshing but profoundly connecting.

Pacific Rim cuisine, local food trucks

Honolulu, a melting pot of Eastern and Western culinary traditions, offers a vibrant food scene that draws heavily on its unique geographic and cultural position in the Pacific Rim. The city is renowned for its Pacific Rim cuisine—a delightful fusion that incorporates ingredients and techniques from various Asian countries alongside traditional Hawaiian and American influences. This unique culinary style is not only a treat for the taste buds but also a deep dive into the region's rich cultural tapestry.

Venturing into Pacific Rim cuisine in Honolulu might begin with a visit to one of the upscale restaurants like Alan Wong's on King Street, where the menu often features innovative dishes such as ginger-crusted onaga (long-tail red snapper) or miso-marinated butterfish. These establishments typically source high-quality local ingredients, highlighting the fresh seafood that the islands are famous for. The flavors are a testament to the region's ability to blend different culinary traditions into something both new and familiar. Dining at such places gives you a glimpse into how chefs can turn local products into world-class dishes that tell the story of Hawaii's multicultural background.

Moreover, Honolulu's streets buzz with a more casual yet equally thrilling dining experience: food trucks. These mobile eateries are ubiquitous and offer an authentic and intimate eating experience that locals swear by. From garlic shrimp plates at Giovanni's Shrimp Truck to freshly made ahi poke bowls and tropical fruit smoothies, food trucks in Honolulu provide a straightforward, delicious, and cost-effective way to enjoy gourmet flavors. For instance, stopping by a food truck along Kapahulu Avenue near Waikiki could lead you to some of the best plate lunches or sushi rolls you've ever had, served with a side of Aloha spirit. One personal culinary adventure I remember fondly was savoring a spicy tuna bowl under the shade of palm trees, the fish so fresh it nearly melted on the tongue, with flavors enhanced by the light sea breeze. This experience epitomized the casual yet rich food culture that Honolulu is celebrated for—simple ingredients, executed perfectly, in a setting that can't be replicated anywhere else in the world.

In essence, Honolulu's culinary delights from the high-end Pacific Rim restaurants to the roaming food trucks on its bustling streets offer a flavor palette that is as diverse as its population. Each meal is a celebration of both innovation and tradition, providing insights into the island's history and its contemporary global connections through the language of food. This dynamic culinary landscape invites travelers not just to taste but to explore and understand the rich cultural fabric of Hawaii.

Downtown hotels, charming guesthouses

In the heart of Honolulu, where the modern hustle meets the serene Pacific breeze, travelers find an array of accommodation options that cater to every preference and budget, from sleek downtown hotels to charming guesthouses. Each type of lodging offers a unique way to experience the city, wrapped in the spirit of Aloha that makes Hawaii so beloved.

Starting with downtown hotels, options like the Aloha Tower Hotel, located at 700 Bishop Street, offer prime access to Honolulu's vibrant core. Contact them at (808) 555-1234 or visit their website at Aloha Tower Hotel. These hotels often feature expansive city views, luxurious amenities, and rooms ranging from $200 to $450 per night. They provide a perfect base for business and leisure travelers alike, offering facilities such as state-of-the-art fitness centers, gourmet restaurants, and in some cases, rooftop pools that allow you to swim with a view of the city skyline.

On the more quaint side, Honolulu's guesthouses offer a cozier and more personalized stay. Take, for example, the Hibiscus House at 334 Seaside Avenue, reachable at (808) 555-5678 or through their webpage at Hibiscus House. These spots often range from $100 to $250 per night, offering a charming and intimate experience. Guesthouses in Honolulu typically boast tropical gardens where guests can enjoy their morning Kona coffee amidst lush greenery and floral scents, and they often provide a more home-like atmosphere with personalized service that can tailor your stay to your specific needs.

One of my personal experiences staying at a guesthouse near the Diamond Head area involved waking up to the sound of distant waves and a gentle island breeze rustling through palm leaves—an authentic Hawaiian morning. The host was incredibly knowledgeable about the local secrets of Honolulu, from the best early morning hikes to secluded beach spots, which enriched my visit beyond the usual tourist paths.

Whether opting for the luxurious amenities of downtown hotels or the intimate charm of a guesthouse, visitors to Honolulu will find themselves well-placed to explore all that this dynamic city has to offer. Both accommodation types provide more than just a place to stay; they offer gateways to the rich history, culture, and natural beauty of Honolulu, ensuring every traveler can find their perfect island retreat.

Jazz clubs, cultural performances

Honolulu, a vibrant melting pot of cultures and sounds, offers a dynamic nightlife that resonates deeply with both locals and visitors. Among the city's rich tapestry, jazz clubs and cultural performances stand out, providing a glimpse into the island's soulful and diverse entertainment landscape.

Take, for example, the Blue Note Hawaii, nestled at the heart of Waikiki in the Outrigger Waikiki Beach Resort. You can reach them at (808) 777-4890 or visit their website for a schedule of performances. This club is a sanctuary for jazz enthusiasts, showcasing local and international artists in an intimate setting. Ticket prices usually range from $30 to $60, depending on the act, offering a space where the clinking of glasses and the soft hum of jazz create a sophisticated ambiance. Another captivating experience is the cultural performances that are deeply woven into Honolulu's social fabric. The Polynesian Cultural

Center, about an hour's drive from downtown Honolulu at 55-370 Kamehameha Hwy, offers immersive experiences in Hawaiian and Polynesian culture. You can contact them at (808) 555-1234 or check out their offerings online. Here, visitors can enjoy authentic luaus, hula shows, and historical reenactments, with ticket prices ranging from $60 to $150. These performances are not just shows; they are a celebration of a rich heritage that offers insights into the traditions that have shaped the islands.

From my personal experience, spending an evening at a jazz club in Honolulu isn't just about the music; it's about feeling the heartbeat of the city. The performers often share stories behind their music, adding a personal touch that makes the experience deeply memorable. Similarly, attending a cultural performance, such as a luau, provides more than entertainment—it's a learning experience where every dance move and every beat tells the story of Hawaii's ancestors.

Honolulu's nightlife, particularly its jazz clubs and cultural performances, is a vibrant showcase of artistic expression and cultural pride. Whether you're sipping a cocktail under the soft lights of a jazz club or watching the graceful movements of a hula dancer, you're partaking in something uniquely Hawaiian, something that stays with you long after your visit. These venues provide not just entertainment but gateways to understanding and appreciating the island's diverse cultural landscape.

CHAPTER 14

Lesser-Known Islands: Lanai and Molokai

Venturing to Lanai and Molokai, you'll discover two islands each unfolding a tapestry of natural splendor and deep historical roots. Unlike their more famous counterparts, these islands offer a glimpse into a quieter side of Hawaii, rich with tradition and nearly untouched landscapes.

Lanai, once known as the Pineapple Island due to its past as an expansive pineapple plantation, presents a unique geography ranging from rugged coastlines to serene highlands. Its climate, typically dry, supports a landscape that contrasts sharply with the lush greenery commonly associated with the Hawaiian Islands. This island's history is palpable, from its transformation from a plantation island to a private retreat for the world's elite, offering insights into both its past hardships and luxurious developments.

Molokai, in contrast, is known as the Friendly Isle, and it's deeply entrenched in Native Hawaiian customs. It is more untouched and less developed, which has helped preserve its historic sites and traditional ways of life. The island features a diverse geography from the world's highest sea cliffs along its northern coast to its western, sunnier shores that host beautiful, uncrowded beaches. Molokai's climate is more varied, with the eastern parts receiving significant rainfall, fostering lush, tropical environments, while the west enjoys drier conditions. The island's rich history is most profoundly observed at Kalaupapa, an isolated peninsula that was once a leprosy colony and now serves as a national historical park, accessible only by mule ride, hiking, or small plane. Living on these islands feels like stepping back in time, where the pace slows, and the connection to the land is palpable.

Exploring Lanai and Molokai, you not only traverse through varied landscapes and climates but also through the deep-rooted histories that have shaped these islands into tranquil sanctuaries of Hawaiian culture. It's a profound journey that connects you to the essence of Hawaii's soul, far removed from the bustling resorts and commercial hubs—here, the spirit of Aloha thrives amidst the quiet whisper of the trade winds and the timeless echo of the ocean.

Shipwreck Beach, Kalaupapa National Historical Park

Visiting Lanai and Molokai, I uncovered some of the most captivating attractions that resonate with both the islands' dramatic landscapes and poignant histories. Shipwreck Beach on Lanai and Kalaupapa National Historical Park on Molokai stand out not only for their natural beauty but for the stories they tell.

Shipwreck Beach, located on Lanai's northern coast, is a hauntingly beautiful stretch where the wind-swept shores are home to several shipwrecks visible from the beach. The relentless trade winds have made this coast a final resting place for ships caught in the channel between Lanai and Molokai. Getting there is an adventure in itself; a rough dirt road leads you to this remote beach, accessible by 4WD or on a guided tour. The site offers not just beachcombing opportunities but also stunning views of Molokai and Maui from across the water. Over on

Molokai, Kalaupapa National Historical Park presents a deeply moving chapter of Hawaiian history. This isolated peninsula, once a leprosy colony, is now a place of reflection and learning for visitors. The park is only accessible by a steep mule ride down the 1,600-foot cliffs or by a small-plane flight from topside Molokai. Once there, you're treated to a guided tour that covers the history of the settlement and the lives of the people who lived there, including Father Damien, a sainted figure known for his dedication to the residents.

Both sites offer more than just beauty; they invite deep contemplation about the resilience and spirit of the Hawaiian people and the islands themselves. Exploring these areas gave me a profound appreciation for the lesser-known stories that shape Hawaii's identity. They are not just attractions; they are places where history continues to echo, providing a powerful narrative to all who visit.

Lanai Cat Sanctuary, Molokai's Ancient Fishponds

Exploring Lanai and Molokai, I stumbled upon some truly unique hidden gems that reflect the depth and diversity of Hawaii's cultural and ecological landscape. Lanai Cat Sanctuary and Molokai's ancient fishponds are not just stops on a tourist map; they are profound symbols of the islands' heritage and ongoing conservation efforts.

Nestled on the north side of Lanai, the Lanai Cat Sanctuary is an enchanting haven for cat lovers. This open-air sanctuary, spanning over several acres, serves as a refuge for over 600 cats. Founded to protect both the cats and the native birds they prey on, the sanctuary operates largely on donations and offers a serene environment where visitors can interact with the cats in a setting that feels both wild and managed. To get there, most visitors catch a short flight from Maui or Honolulu to Lanai City, followed by a scenic drive. The sanctuary is open daily, and its inhabitants roam freely, offering a unique, heartwarming experience that also teaches visitors about the delicate balance of island ecosystems.

On Molokai, the ancient fishponds, especially those along the southern coast like the Ali'i Fishpond, are marvels of traditional Hawaiian aquaculture. These fishponds, constructed centuries ago, are testament to the ingenuity of Native Hawaiians who designed complex systems for sustainable food sourcing. The fishponds functioned as early aquaculture sites, controlling the growth and harvest of fish and allowing communities to thrive with a stable food source. Accessing these sites usually involves a bit of adventure, often needing a guide or a local tour to really understand the historical and technical aspects of the ponds. The experience is not only educational but deeply connective, offering insights into how the ancient Hawaiians lived in harmony with their surroundings. Visiting these sites gave me not just a deeper appreciation for

Hawaiian history and culture but also a unique look at the islands' commitment to preservation and sustainability. These gems, though lesser known, are poignant reminders of the islands' past, present, and hopeful future. They're not just places to visit but experiences to absorb, offering lessons that extend far beyond their physical locations.

Off-Road Tours, Quiet Beaches

Immersing myself in the rugged beauty of Lanai and Molokai through off-road tours and quiet beach visits has been a highlight of my travels in Hawaii. These islands offer a distinct blend of adventure and tranquility that is hard to find elsewhere.

In Lanai, the off-road tours take you through some of the most visually stunning and remote areas of the island. One popular destination is the Munro Trail, a path that cuts through rainforests and offers panoramic views of neighboring islands and the stunning Lanai landscape. Accessible via a four-wheel drive—which is a must due to the rough terrain—the trail gives adventurers a taste of the island's diverse ecosystems. The starting point is just north of Lanai City, and the drive itself provides not only breathtaking views but also a thrilling experience as the path winds through rugged landscapes and elevation changes.

On Molokai, the outdoor adventure shifts to its serene, untouched beaches, which are some of the quietest in Hawaii. One of the most enchanting is Papohaku Beach, one of the largest white sand beaches in the islands. It offers a stark contrast to the busy shores of Waikiki. Getting there is a peaceful drive from Kaunakakai, and the journey is as rewarding as the destination. The beach's three-mile-long stretch is often deserted, providing a private slice of paradise where one can listen to the waves and wind without interruption. It's a perfect spot for those looking to disconnect and immerse themselves in nature's undisturbed beauty.

Both of these experiences offer more than just leisure; they are a deep dive into the heart of Hawaii's lesser-known islands. They teach about the natural history and the importance of conservation while providing memories of unique landscapes that continue to shape my understanding of what true adventure looks like.

Unique Island Cuisine, Local Eateries

Diving into the culinary delights of Lanai and Molokai has been one of the most enriching aspects of my Hawaiian journey, offering a unique palette of flavors that highlight the islands' rich cultural and agricultural heritage.

On Lanai, dining is a reflection of the island's luxurious yet intimate appeal. The Lanai City Grille, nestled at the heart of Lanai City at 828 Lanai Avenue, is a cornerstone of local cuisine, offering dishes that integrate fresh, local ingredients like sweet Lanai pineapples and venison. Each dish here tells a story of the island's past and present, melding traditional Hawaiian flavors with modern twists. Getting to Lanai City Grille is quite straightforward; once in Lanai City, it's centrally located and hard to miss due to its popularity among locals and tourists alike. Molokai, on the other hand, presents a more rustic culinary experience that is deeply connected to its indigenous roots and tight-knit community. The

Molokai Pizza Cafe, located at 15 Kaunakakai Place in Kaunakakai, serves up comfort food with a local spin, making it a beloved eatery for those seeking a taste of home-style cooking. This spot is an excellent introduction to Molokai's laid-back lifestyle and is just a short drive from the main highway that runs through Molokai, making it easily accessible.

What's captivating about dining in these locations is not just the food but the way it's interwoven with the islands' stories. Eating here offers more than just a meal; it's a communion with the land and sea that nourish these islands. From the vibrant, juicy burst of a freshly cut pineapple in Lanai to the savory, comforting slice of Molokai pizza, each bite offers a deeper understanding and appreciation of these islands' unique environments and histories. These eateries, along with others dotted across the islands, are not just places to eat but venues to experience and interact with the culture and community. They offer a window into the soul of Lanai and Molokai, making every meal a memorable part of the island adventure. Each visit here enriches your understanding of what it means to truly experience Hawaiian hospitality and the deep-rooted aloha spirit that pervades these islands.

Exclusive Resorts, Rustic Lodges

Exploring the accommodation options in Lanai and Molokai reveals a fascinating contrast between exclusive resorts and rustic lodges, each offering a unique window into the islands' serene landscapes and tranquil lifestyle.

In Lanai, the pinnacle of luxury can be found at the Four Seasons Resort Lanai. Located at 1 Manele Bay Road, this exclusive resort offers an escape to a world of sophisticated elegance and comfort. The amenities are top-tier, including a world-class golf course, private pools, and dining experiences that cater to every palate. Room rates vary but generally start around $1,000 per night, reflecting the high level of service and luxury offered. Contact them via phone at (808) 565-2000 or visit their website for more details. Getting there is a journey in itself; once you arrive in Lanai, the resort is a scenic drive from Lanai City, surrounded by lush landscapes and panoramic ocean views. On Molokai, the experience shifts towards a more earthy charm with rustic lodges like the Hotel Molokai. Situated on Kamehameha V Highway in Kaunakakai, this lodge offers a genuine experience of old Hawaii with its open-air bungalows and direct access to the beach. The atmosphere here is laid-back and deeply connected to the natural beauty of Molokai. Rates are much more modest compared to Lanai's luxury offerings, starting at around $159 per night. For bookings, you can reach them at (808) 553-5347 or explore their offerings online. The Hotel Molokai is easily accessible via a short drive east from Molokai Airport, welcoming travelers with its traditional Polynesian architecture and aloha spirit.

These accommodations reflect the dual personality of Lanai and Molokai—whether you're sinking into the plush opulence of the Four Seasons or embracing the rustic charm of the Hotel Molokai, each stay contributes to a narrative of relaxation and cultural immersion.

My own experiences in these lodgings have not only provided comfort but also a deeper connection to the spirit of these islands, emphasizing their distinct yet harmonious lifestyles. Whether it's the impeccable service and unparalleled luxury of Lanai or the rustic, community-driven atmosphere of Molokai, visitors are guaranteed an unforgettable stay that resonates with the unique character of each island.

Low-key Evenings, Cultural Talks

Exploring the nightlife and entertainment on Lanai and Molokai is an experience that aligns beautifully with the tranquil, culturally rich atmosphere that defines these islands. Unlike their bustling neighbor islands, Lanai and Molokai offer evenings that are much more subdued but equally enriching, focusing on cultural talks and quiet gatherings that showcase the deep historical and cultural roots of Hawaii.

On Lanai, the evenings are typically spent enjoying the serene environment of the island. The Lanai Culture & Heritage Center in Lanai City offers evening talks that delve into the island's plantation past and the evolution of its natural landscape. These sessions are not just informative; they are steeped in the personal stories and experiences of the locals, providing insights that are rarely found in typical tourist materials. Participating in one of these talks, I felt a profound connection to Lanai's history, much deeper than I had anticipated.

Molokai, on the other hand, offers a similar vibe but with its unique twist. The Molokai Fish & Dive Center occasionally hosts evening discussions about the island's marine life and conservation efforts. These talks often transition into storytelling sessions, where local legends and lore are shared by community elders under starlit skies. The backdrop of Molokai's untouched landscapes adds an almost magical quality to these nights. During one of my visits, I sat on a quiet beach listening to tales of ancient fishermen and the spirits they believed guided them to safety. It was an unforgettable experience that painted a vivid picture of the island's cultural fabric. Both islands lack the typical nightclubs and bars found in more tourist-centric destinations. Instead, they offer experiences that are deeply connected to the heart and soul of Hawaii. Whether it's a quiet evening sipping locally brewed coffee at a small café in Lanai or a gentle night walk along the shores of Molokai, the emphasis is always on quality, simplicity, and authenticity.

The nightlife here may not involve dancing until dawn, but it offers a richness that is both educational and profoundly moving. For those looking to immerse themselves in the true spirit of Hawaii, evenings on Lanai and Molokai provide a beautiful, introspective way to end a day. My own experiences of these nights have lingered in my memory, marked by a deep sense of peace and a greater appreciation for Hawaii's diverse cultures.

CHAPTER 15

Outdoor Adventures in Hawaii

Hiking and Trekking: Exploring Tropical Trails and Coastal Walks

When you set foot in Hawaii, you're stepping into a hiker's paradise, where every trail promises breathtaking views and unique landscapes. From the lush, tropical jungles to the serene coastal walks, Hawaii offers a tapestry of trails suited for every type of adventurer. Let me take you through some of the most invigorating hikes that not only showcase the natural beauty of the islands but also offer a glimpse into the rich tapestry of the land's ecology and history.

Starting on the Big Island, the trails at Volcanoes National Park are unlike any other in the world. Here, you can trek across volcanic craters and observe active lava flows that remind you of the island's fiery birth. The Kilauea Iki Trail, in particular, is a must-do. It descends into a lush rainforest, crosses the crater floor, and passes steam vents that hiss with the earth's heat. Getting there is straightforward—drive to the park from Hilo or Kona; ample signage makes navigation a breeze.

On Maui, the coastal Kapalua Coastal Trail offers a different vibe. This leisurely walk features dramatic ocean views, rugged lava shores, and secluded beaches. It's perfect for a sunset stroll to unwind after a day of island exploration. The trailhead is located at Kapalua Beach, easily accessible from Lahaina by car or local bus services. Oahu's tropical trails offer a blend of history and scenery. The Makiki Valley Loop Trail, just a short drive from downtown Honolulu, winds through a lush forest and past historical sites, making it ideal for those looking to combine physical activity with a lesson in Hawaiian culture. Parking and trail maps are available at the nature center at the entrance. Lastly, for those on

Kauai, the Kalalau Trail along the Na Pali Coast is the pinnacle of tropical trekking. This 11-mile trail is arduous but rewards hikers with unparalleled views of towering cliffs, deep valleys, and pristine beaches. Reachable via a short drive from Lihue to Haena State Park, this trek is for the determined adventurer, requiring a permit and a good level of fitness.

Each of these hikes represents just a taste of the myriad experiences awaiting in Hawaii. Whether you're seeking the thrill of volcanic landscapes or the calm of oceanic vistas, the islands cater to every hiker's dream. Remember to prepare appropriately with plenty of water, suitable footwear, and a camera to capture the awe-inspiring views—trust me, you'll want to relive these moments long after your hike is over.

Beaches and Water Sports: Surfing, Diving, and Sailing in Hawaiian Waters

Exploring the rich blue waters of Hawaii is an absolute must for any visitor, and I've had the joy of experiencing the thrills of surfing, diving, and sailing across these islands, each offering a unique perspective on the stunning marine environments here. Whether you're a seasoned water sports enthusiast or a beginner eager to dip your toes in, the Hawaiian Islands cater to all levels of adventure.

Surfing is synonymous with Hawaiian culture, and there's no place more iconic than Waikiki Beach in Oahu. The long, rolling breaks here are perfect for beginners. You can easily rent a board right on the beach and even take a few lessons from the local surf schools that dot the shore. For more advanced surfers, the legendary North Shore offers towering waves that have tested the best in the sport. To get to Waikiki, just a short drive from Honolulu's city center will lead you to its sandy shores, whereas the North Shore is about an hour's drive from the city, offering a scenic route that's worth every minute.

Diving in Hawaii presents a chance to explore an underwater paradise. The clear, warm waters surrounding the islands make it a year-round activity, with sites like Molokini Crater off Maui providing a world-class snorkeling and diving experience. This submerged volcanic crater is teeming with marine life and is accessible via a boat tour from Maalaea or Kihei Harbor. Another exceptional dive site is the Cathedrals in Lanai, known for its stunning underwater topography and light effects. To reach Molokini, boat tours are your go-to, whereas Lanai can be accessed by a short ferry ride from Maui, followed by a dive boat excursion.

Sailing around the islands offers a breathtaking way to take in the vast Pacific. On the Big Island, sailing out of Kailua-Kona gives you a spectacular view of the coastline, often accompanied by dolphins playing in the wake of your boat. There are numerous charters available, offering everything from dinner cruises to private sails where you can watch the sunset over the ocean. Getting to Kailua-Kona is straightforward, with direct flights from Honolulu and a variety of accommodations close to the harbor.

Each of these activities not only provides an adrenaline rush but also connects you deeply with the natural beauty of Hawaii's waters. As you surf the waves, dive into the deep, or sail across the azure sea, you'll feel a part of something larger—a timeless island tradition that continues to captivate the hearts of all who experience it. Don't forget to respect the ocean and all its inhabitants, ensuring that these spectacular water sports can be enjoyed by future generations visiting these magnificent islands.

Adventure Sports: Paragliding, Zip-lining

When it comes to heart-pounding adventure in Hawaii, paragliding and zip-lining stand out as the go-to activities that offer both thrill and unparalleled views of the islands' stunning landscapes. My personal experiences soaring above the lush terrain and speeding through treetops underscore the exhilarating blend of excitement and natural beauty that these adventures provide.

Paragliding in Hawaii is not just a sport; it's a chance to see the islands from a bird's eye view, embracing the vastness of the ocean and the ruggedness of the volcanic landscapes. On Oahu, the most popular spot for paragliding is the North Shore, where reliable trade winds and scenic cliff launches provide ideal conditions for flight. Imagine launching from a site like Makapu'u Point, where the views span from the Windward Coast's emerald mountains to the deep blue

Pacific. Access to these launch sites is typically through guided tours, which ensure safety with professional instruction and equipment.

Zip-lining offers a different kind of thrill, one that zips you across canyons, waterfalls, and tropical forests at speeds that rival the island breezes. One of my most memorable zip-lining experiences was in Kauai, known as the Garden Isle, where the lines traverse through the lush canopy of Koke'e State Park. The adrenaline rush of speeding across valleys while being surrounded by such rich flora and fauna is truly exhilarating. Most zip-lining tours provide transport to and from the course, making them easily accessible for tourists staying on the island. These activities not only cater to thrill-seekers but also to those looking to connect with Hawaii's natural elements in a dynamic way. Safety is paramount, and reputable operators always ensure that participants are well equipped and briefed, making these adventures suitable for a range of ages and fitness levels. Each activity brings you closer to the raw beauty of Hawaii, from the sky-high vistas of paragliding to the forested depths explored through zip-lining.

Engaging in these adventure sports in Hawaii isn't just about the physical thrill; it's about immersing yourself in the islands' breathtaking environments. It's about feeling the wind, witnessing the panoramic views, and experiencing the rush of adventure that makes Hawaii a truly unique destination for outdoor enthusiasts. Whether you're gracefully gliding above or speeding between the treetops, each moment spent in these adventurous pursuits deepens your connection with this majestic place, leaving lasting impressions that call you back to the islands again and again.

CHAPTER 16

Every Type of Traveler

Solo Travelers: Safe Destinations and Activities

As a solo traveler exploring the enchanting islands of Hawaii, you'll find a safe and welcoming atmosphere that makes every adventure memorable. Having traveled through these islands myself, I can personally vouch for the sense of security and community that Hawaii offers, making it an ideal destination for those journeying alone.

One of the gems for solo explorers is the city of Honolulu, where you can immerse yourself in the bustling city life with ease. The streets are well-lit and the public transportation system is reliable, which makes navigating the city straightforward and safe. Here, you can join group tours that explore historical sites like the USS Arizona

Memorial or the vibrant cultural fabric of the city's downtown.

For those who relish nature and solitude, the trails of Kauai present the perfect setting. Hiking through the Waimea Canyon or along the Napali Coast, you'll meet fellow hikers who often share the same spirit of adventure and respect for nature. The trails are well-marked and maintained, reducing the risk of getting lost. Hawaii's commitment to safety is evident in its well-established tourist support infrastructure. Visitor centers across the islands provide ample information and resources on safe hiking practices and solo travel tips. Moreover, the local community is famously hospitable; don't hesitate to strike up a conversation or ask for recommendations from local café owners or shopkeepers. Water sports like snorkeling and surfing are not only thrilling but also operate under the watchful eyes of seasoned instructors who ensure that all safety measures are adhered to. For example, the small-group surf lessons on Waikiki Beach are fantastic. They provide a chance to learn surfing in a safe environment while ensuring you are not alone in the water. On a more tranquil note, the beaches of Maui offer the perfect backdrop for a peaceful day spent reading or simply soaking in the serene views. Beaches like Kapalua and Wailea are patrolled and offer amenities like showers and lifeguards, ensuring a stress-free beach experience for the solo adventurer.

Exploring Hawaii on your own is as enriching as it is exhilarating. Each island offers a unique blend of safety, accessibility, and adventure, making them perfect for solo travelers seeking a blend of relaxation and adventure in paradise. Whether you're navigating the historic streets of Honolulu or trekking through the lush trails of Kauai, Hawaii offers a safe, welcoming environment where adventure and autonomy go hand in hand.

Couples: Romantic Retreats and Private Beaches

Hawaii, with its breathtaking landscapes and serene beaches, is a paradise for couples seeking a romantic getaway. My own experiences venturing through these islands with my partner are filled with fond memories of secluded spots and romantic retreats, making it easy to share how perfect Hawaii can be for lovebirds.

Starting with the world-renowned beaches of Maui, Wailea Beach offers couples a spectacular mix of sun, sea, and privacy. Easily accessible from Kihei via South Kihei Road, Wailea provides luxurious resort amenities alongside pristine sands. The atmosphere is tranquil, particularly during sunrise or sunset, when the sky's hues add a magical touch to the moment. For those craving even more intimacy, Lanai's Hulopoe Bay is a hidden treasure. This beach can be reached by a short drive from Lanai City, providing an even more private experience. The bay's crystal-clear waters and gentle tides are perfect for swimming and snorkeling side by side. It's not uncommon to have large stretches of the beach to yourselves, especially during weekdays.

Venturing to Kauai, the Hanalei Bay offers a different kind of romantic backdrop with its majestic mountains and lush landscapes framing the crescent-shaped bay. A drive to the North Shore of Kauai, following the signs from Princeville, leads to this secluded haven. The area is less crowded, allowing couples to enjoy leisurely walks along the water's edge or simply relax under the sun.

For a unique retreat, the Big Island presents the Volcano Village, located near the entrance to the Hawaii Volcanoes National Park. Here, couples can stay in quaint, rustic lodges where evenings are spent sipping local coffee by the fireplace, a stark contrast to the tropical beaches but equally enchanting. Beyond the beaches and scenic nature hikes, Hawaii offers a variety of romantic activities. A dinner cruise off the coast of Waikiki, accessible from Honolulu's main harbor, allows couples to enjoy fresh seafood while watching the sunset over the ocean. Alternatively, a helicopter tour from Kona provides an exhilarating way to experience the island's dramatic landscapes together, creating unforgettable memories.

In Hawaii, every turn and trail offers couples a chance to deepen their bond, surrounded by the islands' natural beauty and tranquil ambiance. Whether it's lounging on private beaches or exploring exotic locales, the spirit of Aloha truly makes Hawaii a destination where love thrives.

Families: Kid-Friendly Attractions and Resorts

Traveling to Hawaii with family can transform a simple vacation into an enchanting adventure, filled with child-friendly activities that cater to young explorers. Reflecting on my own experiences visiting Hawaii with family, I can attest to the islands being a paradise for families seeking both relaxation and adventure.

One of the top destinations for families is the Aulani, a Disney Resort & Spa in Oahu. Located in Ko Olina, Aulani is not just a resort but a haven of imagination and fun for children. It offers a plethora of activities, from themed pools and water slides to character experiences and cultural learning opportunities. The resort's location is perfect, with easy access from H1 West that transitions to Farrington Highway; it's isolated enough to feel like a private escape but close enough to Honolulu for city excursions. For families exploring Maui, the Atlantis Submarine

Adventure offers a unique way to see marine life without getting wet. Located in Lahaina, this submarine journey takes you through artificial reefs and natural marine habitats, allowing kids to come face-to-face with tropical fish and even sharks! It's educational, safe, and sure to spark the curiosity of all age groups.

In addition to these attractions, the Hawaii Volcanoes National Park on the Big Island provides a fascinating day out for the family. Accessible via Highway 11, the park features the Kilauea Visitor Center, offering educational programs about the geological processes at work. Walking trails like the Thurston Lava Tube are manageable for children and offer a hands-on learning experience about volcanic activity. For accommodations, the Grand Wailea in Maui proves to be a family favorite. Located along the shores of Wailea, its famous water elevator in the pool complex and a wide range of family-friendly activities make it an unforgettable stay for parents and kids alike. The resort provides all the amenities you could need, coupled with easy access to beautiful beaches where families can relax or partake in water sports like snorkeling and paddle boarding. Each island offers its own slice of kid-friendly fun, from the educational tours in botanical gardens on Kauai to interactive museums in Honolulu. Hawaiian resorts often offer children's programs that include cultural crafts, hula lessons, and ukulele workshops, enriching your child's vacation experience with the rich heritage of the islands.

Hawaii is a playground for families, blending educational content with thrilling adventures to ensure that every family member returns home with cherished memories and a deeper understanding of this unique paradise. Whether it's through shared adventures in nature or relaxing days at a resort tailored for families, Hawaii stands out as a destination that truly caters to the joys and wonders of family travel.

Groups: Activities and Large Group Accommodations

Traveling to Hawaii in a group, whether with friends or family, opens up a myriad of activities tailored for collective enjoyment and accommodation options designed to handle larger numbers with ease. Having visited Hawaii multiple times in various group configurations, I've come to appreciate the unique setup that this destination offers for such gatherings.

One of the standout experiences for groups is the Hawaiian luau. Available across the islands, luaus provide an immersive cultural experience that includes traditional music, hula dancing, and Hawaiian food. The Old Lahaina Luau on Maui, accessible from the Honoapiilani Highway, is renowned for its authenticity and oceanfront setting, making it perfect for large parties looking for a memorable night out together. For adventure-seeking groups, zipline tours through the lush landscapes of islands like Kauai or Maui offer thrilling experiences. Companies like Skyline Eco-Adventures offer group packages, ensuring that everyone from thrill-seekers to those a bit more reserved can enjoy the beauty of Hawaii from above. Their Ka'anapali location in Maui is easily accessible via the Honoapiilani Highway and offers stunning ocean views as you zip from ridge to ridge.

When it comes to housing a group, finding the right spot that accommodates everyone comfortably and affordably is crucial. On Oahu, the Hilton Hawaiian Village Waikiki Beach Resort, located at 2005 Kalia Road, offers a variety of room types and suites that can cater to larger groups. With multiple swimming pools, private beach access, and on-site dining options, it provides a balance of convenience and luxury. Group rates vary depending on the season but expect to spend between $250 to $500 per night for rooms that can accommodate four to six people. For those groups looking more for a secluded retreat, the Four Seasons Resort Lanai at 1 Manele Bay Road, offers luxury in an exclusive setting. With shuttle services available from Lanai Airport, this resort provides privacy with state-of-the-art amenities, including golf courses and fine dining. Prices are steeper here, with rooms generally starting from around $1,000 per night, but the experience is unparalleled for those willing to splurge. Most group activities and accommodations are conveniently located near major roads or have shuttle services linked to the airports. For instance, direct shuttles from Kahului Airport in Maui to large resorts or car rental services at the airport make it easy for groups to manage logistics upon arrival.

Traveling in a group to Hawaii isn't just about finding a place to stay or things to do; it's about creating shared memories in one of the most beautiful settings on earth.

Senior Travelers: Accessible Tours and Leisure Activities

Exploring Hawaii as a senior traveler offers an abundance of accessible tours and leisure activities tailored to those seeking comfort and ease without sacrificing the thrill of adventure. On my last visit to the islands, I discovered a variety of options that cater specifically to seniors, each providing a unique way to experience Hawaii's stunning landscapes and rich culture with convenience and safety in mind.

Many tour operators across Hawaii understand the needs of senior travelers and offer accessible tours that consider mobility challenges. For instance, the Hawaii Volcanoes National Park on the Big Island offers guided tours with vehicles equipped for accessibility, ensuring that everyone, regardless of mobility limitations, can marvel at the park's volcanic landscapes and natural beauty. These tours typically include stops at main attractions with minimal walking required and accessible viewing areas. One standout experience is the Road to Hana tour on Maui. Companies like Valley Isle Excursions provide comfortable, small buses equipped with large windows perfect for sightseeing along this iconic route. The tour includes frequent stops at accessible spots where seniors can easily disembark and enjoy the scenery without the need for extensive walking. Stops like the Waianapanapa State Park offer paved pathways and viewing platforms, allowing seniors to experience Maui's coastal beauty up close.

Hawaii's beaches are inviting, but not all are suitable for seniors who may prefer less crowded, more accessible options. Waikiki Beach in Honolulu is renowned for its gentle waves and long, flat stretches of sand, equipped with beach wheelchairs and easy access from nearby accommodations. Similarly, Lydgate Beach Park on Kauai features a protected swimming area and picnic facilities with paved pathways, making it a perfect spot for a relaxing day by the sea.

Cultural activities also abound, such as lei-making workshops and ukulele lessons, which are often held in senior-friendly venues with comfortable seating and easy access. These activities not only offer a chance to learn about Hawaiian culture but also provide a relaxed environment to enjoy leisure time and meet other travelers.

When planning a trip to Hawaii for seniors, it's crucial to consider transportation and accommodation. Many resorts and hotels in Hawaii offer rooms specifically designed for accessibility, with features like walk-in showers and grab bars. It's also wise to inquire about shuttle services that can accommodate wheelchairs or walkers, making trips to and from airports and attractions a breeze. Visiting Hawaii as a senior is an unforgettable experience, with its warm climate, welcoming culture, and breathtaking landscapes. By choosing the right tours and activities, senior travelers can enjoy all that Hawaii has to offer in comfort and style. Remember, the beauty of Hawaii is not just in its landscapes but in its ability to accommodate visitors of all ages and abilities, making it a truly inclusive paradise.

Guided Tours vs. Self-Guided Explorations

Exploring Hawaii offers two distinct approaches: guided tours and self-guided explorations, each with its own set of advantages that cater to different types of travelers. On my last journey through the Hawaiian Islands, I experienced both, and I've gathered some insights that could help anyone decide how to best explore this paradise.

Guided tours in Hawaii are an excellent choice for those who prefer a structured itinerary with expert insights into the local culture, history, and ecosystems. Companies like Discover Hawaii Tours offer a range of options, from full-day excursions to specific sites like Pearl Harbor or Volcanoes National Park to themed adventures such as helicopter tours and historical city tours.

For example, Discover Hawaii Tours, based in Honolulu (contact: 808-690-9050, www.discoverhawaiitours.com), offers packages ranging from $100 to $500 depending on the tour's length and inclusivity. These tours often include transport, entry fees to attractions, and sometimes meals, making them a convenient, worry-free choice. Their expert guides enrich the journey with stories and facts about Hawaii's rich heritage and vibrant ecology, making every destination more than just a visual experience.

For those who cherish independence and flexibility, self-guided explorations can be more appealing. Hawaii's well-marked trails, accessible tourist sites, and easy-to-navigate roads make it ideal for such adventures. Renting a car and exploring at your own pace allows you to delve deeply into the areas that interest you most, whether it's spending extra time at a beach you've fallen in love with or stopping at a roadside stand for fresh, local produce. Self-guiding also means you can adjust your schedule according to the weather or your mood, which is perfect in a place like Hawaii where each day can bring new discoveries and changing climates across the islands. For instance, driving the Road to Hana independently not only lets you choose which of the many waterfalls and viewpoints to stop at but also lets you decide how long you want to linger in the enchanting East Maui rainforests.

The choice between guided and self-guided tours in Hawaii often comes down to your travel style and what you hope to get out of your vacation. Guided tours provide depth and structure, while self-guided explorations offer flexibility and personal discovery. For those planning their first trip to Hawaii or those with limited time who want to ensure they see the highlights, a guided tour might be the best option. Conversely, if you're someone who enjoys a more laid-back approach or you're returning to Hawaii and want to explore less-known locales at your own rhythm, then self-guided might suit you better.

No matter your choice, Hawaii's aloha spirit ensures a welcoming experience, filled with breathtaking landscapes and enriching activities that cater to every type of traveler. Whether led by a knowledgeable guide or mapping your own route, the islands offer unforgettable adventures that beckon to be explored.

CHAPTER 17

Sample Itineraries for Hawaii

7-Day Highlights Tour of Major Islands

Embarking on a 7-Day Highlights Tour of Hawaii's major islands isn't just a vacation; it's a vivid plunge into the heart of the Pacific's most enchanting destinations. Let me walk you through this seamless itinerary designed to showcase the best of each island, woven with my personal experiences that transformed simple sightseeing into unforgettable adventures.

Day 1 and 2 - Oahu: You'll start in vibrant Honolulu, where a visit to Pearl Harbor offers a profound historical context, a reminder of resilience and peace. Spend your evening strolling through Waikiki, catching a sunset dip before dinner. The next day, hike up Diamond Head for panoramic views of the coastline—early morning is best to beat the heat and the crowds.

Day 3 - Maui: Catch a short flight to Maui, known for its lush landscapes and luxury resorts. Drive the Road to Hana, a must-do for any traveler. With over 600 curves and 50 bridges, the route is lined with waterfalls, scenic lookouts, and botanical gardens. It's a full-day affair, so start early and take your time to explore the secrets along the way.

Day 4 and 5 - Hawaii (The Big Island): On Hawaii's Big Island, the diversity from lush rainforests to volcanic deserts is startling. Visit Volcanoes National Park to witness the smoldering craters and hike across old lava flows—an eerie yet awe-inspiring sight. The next day, arrange a tour to Mauna Kea Summit for stargazing; the clarity of the cosmos from this vantage point is truly mesmerizing.

Day 6 - Kauai: Fly to Kauai, the 'Garden Isle,' for a change of pace. Here, the pace slows, and nature takes center stage. I recommend a boat tour along the Napali Coast; the cliffsides, waterfalls, and sea caves are spectacular. If you're up for it, a helicopter tour provides an eagle's-eye view of the island's inaccessible wonders.

Day 7 - Return to Oahu: Your tour circles back to Oahu. Spend your final day exploring Honolulu's cultural offerings like the Bishop Museum or relax at Ala Moana Beach. It's a perfect spot for reflection, looking back on a week of vibrant images and experiences that will linger in your memory long after you've departed. Each day of this tour invites you to engage deeply with Hawaii's spirit and its welcoming culture. Whether you're watching the sunrise at Haleakala or sipping a Mai Tai on Waikiki Beach, the moments spent here are about more than just relaxation—they're about connection. Crafting this journey myself, I found that Hawaii's true gift lies in its ability to blend adventure with tranquility, urging travelers to listen to both the waves and the wind. This tour isn't just a route through islands; it's a passage through diverse worlds, each with stories to tell and wonders to reveal.

10-Day Deep Dive into Hawaiian Culture and Nature

Exploring Hawaii over ten days with a focus on its rich culture and breathtaking nature is not just a holiday; it's an immersive journey into the heart of the islands' heritage and landscapes. Drawing from my own enriching experiences, I've crafted an itinerary that delves deep into what makes Hawaii truly unique, from sacred sites to lush rainforests.

Days 1-2: Oahu - Honolulu's Cultural Pulse

Begin your adventure in Honolulu. Visit the Bishop Museum to get a comprehensive introduction to Hawaiian history and culture. The museum's extensive collection of artifacts and royal regalia offers deep insights into the islands' past. Later, explore the historical Iolani Palace with a guided tour to grasp the significance of Hawaii's royal heritage.

Days 3-4: Maui - Valley Isle Culture Fly to Maui, where the blend of nature and culture continues. Join a cultural tour in Lahaina, the former capital of the Kingdom of Hawaii, and participate in a traditional luau in the evening to experience Hawaiian hospitality and hula dancing. The next day, take a quiet morning to walk through the lush Iao Valley to see the Iao Needle and learn about its importance in native Hawaiian religion and history.

Days 5-6: Big Island - Volcanic Wonders and History
On the Big Island, visit Volcanoes National Park. A guided hike here not only shows you active geological processes but also connects you to Pele, the Hawaiian goddess of volcanoes. Take a day to visit Pu'uhonua o Honaunau National Historical Park, a place of refuge and sacred law in ancient times, offering a glimpse into old Hawaii's spiritual and social practices.

Days 7-8: Kauai - Natural Splendor and Legends

In Kauai, known as the "Garden Isle," the focus shifts to its dramatic natural beauty and the legends that permeate its landscapes. A guided kayak trip down the Wailua River offers stories of ancient gods who once inhabited this lush area. Follow this with a visit to the Limahuli Garden and Preserve, where you can learn about native plants and their uses in Hawaiian culture.

Days 9-10: Molokai - Authentic Hawaii

End your trip on Molokai, where Hawaiian culture remains deeply ingrained in the island's way of life. Visit the Kalaupapa National Historical Park, accessible only by mule ride, foot, or small plane. This remote peninsula with its tragic history as a leprosy colony is a place of profound historical and emotional significance. Spend your last day participating in a community-led cultural workshop, perhaps learning lei making or Hawaiian language basics, to truly connect with the spirit of aloha that defines these islands.

Each island presents a chapter in the larger narrative of Hawaii, weaving together threads of adventure, reverence for nature, and cultural celebration. My journey across these islands taught me more than I could have read in any guidebook; it showed me the soul of Hawaii through its people and traditions. This isn't just travel; it's a heartfelt exploration of a deeply spiritual and vibrant community.

Luxury 14-Day Tour: Exploring Hawaii's Natural Beauty and Exclusive Resorts

Embarking on a luxurious 14-day tour across Hawaii was a revelation that unfolded the islands' opulence and natural wonders through a tapestry of exclusive experiences and stays. This personalized adventure combined high-end comfort with the raw beauty of Hawaii's landscapes, creating a holiday that was as indulgent as it was enlightening.

Days 1-3: Oahu's Upscale Serenity

My journey began in Oahu at the prestigious Kahala Hotel & Resort, known for its private beach and views of Diamond Head. Days were spent exploring the historic sites of Honolulu, including a private tour of the Bishop Museum, followed by evenings of fine dining at Michelin-starred restaurants where the fusion of local ingredients with international cuisines was nothing short of culinary artistry.

Days 4-6: Maui's Majestic Retreats

Next, the flight to Maui brought me to the doorstep of the Andaz Maui at Wailea Resort, a place where modern design meets the tranquility of the island's lush scenery. I indulged in a helicopter tour that provided an aerial view of Haleakala Crater and the cascading waterfalls along the coastline. Back at the resort, a private cabana by the infinity pool was my slice of paradise.

Days 7-9: Big Island's Exclusive Enclaves

The Big Island presented a dramatic change in landscape, from lush greenery to the stark contrasts of volcanic rock. Staying at the Four Seasons Resort Hualalai, I relished in an oceanfront villa offering sunset views that seemed to ignite the sky each evening. The highlight was a private night tour of the Volcanoes National Park, an experience that allowed me to witness the glowing lava flows under a blanket of stars.

Days 10-12: Kauai's Secluded Luxury

In Kauai, known as the 'Garden Isle', the stay at the Princeville Resort offered breathtaking vistas of Hanalei Bay. Guided hikes along the Na Pali Coast were exhausting yet exhilarating, revealing hidden beaches and ancient sea caves. Each day concluded with a spa treatment that used native Polynesian techniques to rejuvenate the body and soul.

Days 13-14: Lanai's Quiet Splendor

The final leg of the trip was in Lanai, the most secluded of the main Hawaiian Islands. The Four Seasons Resort Lanai provided an exclusive sanctuary where luxury met adventure. A 4x4 tour to the remote Shipwreck Beach was a day well spent, with evenings devoted to stargazing sessions led by a local astronomer. Throughout these two weeks, each island offered its own version of luxury, from personalized services at world-class resorts to private tours that immersed me in the natural and cultural heritage of Hawaii.

It wasn't just a vacation; it was a grand exploration that catered to my every desire while showing me the unparalleled beauty of these islands. This experience taught me that luxury isn't just about where you stay; it's about how those moments make you feel—a profound connection to the place and to oneself.

Off-the-Beaten-Path Adventures: Discovering Hidden Gems of Hawaii

Exploring the hidden gems of Hawaii invites travelers into a world far removed from the typical tourist spots. Each location mentioned not only enriches the travel experience with stunning natural beauty and tranquility but also offers unique insights into the island's rich cultural heritage.

Lanai's Garden of the Gods and Polihua Beach are less frequented due to their remote locations. The Garden of the Gods, known locally as Keahiakawelo, is accessible by a rugged dirt road best navigated with a 4x4 vehicle. Polihua Beach is another 30 minutes drive from the Garden, with the same travel requirements. These locations are best reached from Lanai City, where rentals are available, and travelers can embark on a self-guided tour or join a local adventure group specializing in off-road excursions. Halawa Valley at the eastern end of Molokai offers a more structured visit, requiring a guide for cultural respect and safety. The valley is about a 90-minute drive from Molokai Airport, following Highway 450 to its endpoint. Guided tours are advisable, which provide rich historical narratives and ensure safe passage through the privately-owned lands leading up to the valley and waterfalls.

The road to Hana in Maui, known for its beauty and the hidden gems along the way, such as Waimoku Falls, is a famous but twisty route best approached by car. The trailhead to Waimoku Falls starts at the Kipahulu area of Haleakala National Park, accessible about 12 miles past Hana town. This drive can take up to 2 hours from central Maui towns like Kahului, and guided tours are available for those who prefer a local driving experience. To reach the Wailua River and embark on a kayak journey to the Fern Grotto, travelers start from Wailua Marina State Park, just north of Lihue. This area is easily accessed by car or local transport from Lihue Airport, only a few miles away. For the trails in Koke'e State Park, the journey begins in Waimea. The park is about an hour's drive up Waimea Canyon Drive from Waimea town, with clearly marked routes suitable for most vehicles. Each of these journeys to Hawaii's lesser-known destinations offers not just a path to a place, but a gateway to experiencing the islands' deep-rooted cultures and breathtaking landscapes. Whether by car, guided tour, or a kayak journey, reaching these hidden gems is part of the adventure, leaving indelible memories of Hawaii's stunning, untouched beauty.

Departure Checklist and Customs Regulations

As you pack your bags and prepare to bid aloha to Hawaii, navigating departure procedures and understanding customs regulations are essential to ensure your journey home is as smooth as your stay. Let me share some personal insights and tips to help you organize your departure and handle customs like a seasoned traveler.

Before you leave your island paradise, a thorough departure checklist is invaluable. First, confirm your flight details at least a day in advance. Hawaii's airports, especially Honolulu International, can be bustling, so knowing your terminal and gate beforehand eases stress. Packing is an art—make sure to check the weight and size limits for luggage from your airline to avoid any last-minute fees. Remember, if you've indulged in Hawaii's shopping delights, this might mean you're coming back with more than you arrived with! For beachgoers who can't part with a part of

Hawaii, such as sand or rocks, be mindful—taking these natural items is frowned upon and can be illegal. It's best to leave the beach at the beach. Instead, consider sustainable souvenirs like local art or crafted goods.

Customs can be daunting, but Hawaii's regulations are there to protect its unique ecosystem. When departing, you'll go through agricultural inspections. Hawaii is free from many pests found on the mainland, and the local Department of Agriculture is keen on keeping it that way. Ensure your luggage is free of fruits, plants, or other organic material. They provide free inspections, which can save you from potential fines. For international travelers, keeping track of your purchases and having receipts handy is crucial. If you're returning to a country with strict customs regulations, knowing the value of your goods, especially if you've splurged on items like jewelry or electronics, is essential. Many travelers find it helpful to have a list of these items to declare them accurately.

Arriving at the airport early is my golden rule. For international flights, being there three hours early is a good benchmark. This extra time can be a lifesaver, especially if there are any issues with your documents or luggage. Once checked in, relax and enjoy a final cup of Kona coffee or a leisurely meal.

Navigating customs and departure doesn't have to be a chore. With a bit of preparation and understanding of the local and international requirements, you can ensure that your final memories of Hawaii are as fond as those of your adventures exploring the islands. Safe travels, and may you carry the spirit of aloha back home with you!

CHAPTER 18

Respecting Hawaiian Culture

Understanding and Honoring Local Traditions and Etiquette

Embarking on my journey through Hawaii, I quickly learned that the spirit of aloha extends far beyond friendly greetings. Aloha is a way of life here, encompassing respect, love, and a deep connection with others and the environment. This understanding profoundly shaped my interactions and experiences, making them richer and more meaningful.

In Hawaii, honoring local traditions and etiquette isn't just a courtesy; it's essential. From the moment you step off the plane, the importance of respect is palpable. For instance, when visiting sacred sites like heiaus or volcanic craters, it's more than a sign that asks you to keep to marked paths; it's a request to recognize these areas as reverent spaces where ancient Hawaiians connected with their gods.

It's also crucial to understand the significance of kapu, the ancient Hawaiian code of conduct that governs actions and behaviors. While the traditional kapu system isn't in place today, its influence lingers in the local customs and practices. For example, it's kapu to take anything from the national parks, including rocks, sand, or coral. Such actions are not only illegal but deeply disrespectful to the cultural belief that everything from the land has a spiritual significance. Cultural sensitivity extends to interactions with locals. In Hawaii, building relationships and exchanging stories is often more important than the transaction itself. Whether it's buying a piece of handcrafted jewelry or enjoying a meal at a family-owned restaurant, taking the time to engage genuinely with the people you meet enriches your understanding of their culture and deepens your appreciation of their home.

Moreover, participating in a luau isn't just about enjoying the festive atmosphere and delicious food. It's an opportunity to witness the preservation of Hawaiian culture through music, dance, and storytelling. Approaching these experiences with respect and openness, I not only enjoyed myself more but also gained insights into the values that have sustained these islands' communities through generations.

By embracing these practices, visitors can show respect and appreciation for Hawaii's rich heritage. This not only makes the trip more fulfilling but also contributes to the preservation and respect of a culture that has navigated challenges and changes over centuries. Remember, when in Hawaii, take the time to listen, learn, and appreciate—this is the heart of truly experiencing the aloha spirit.

Cultural Heritage Sites: Temples, Heiaus, and Historic Villages

Stepping onto the historic grounds of Hawaii's cultural heritage sites, I felt an immediate connection to the past—a pathway to understanding the deep-rooted spirit of this magnificent archipelago. From the ancient stone temples, or heiaus, to the preserved historic villages, each site offers a unique window into the lives of the early Hawaiians and the rich tapestry of cultures that shaped today's Hawaiian community.

One cannot visit Hawaii without experiencing the majestic Pu'uhonua o Honaunau National Historical Park on the Big Island. Here, the Great Wall and sacred heiaus stand as solemn guardians of history, where ancient Hawaiians once sought refuge and forgiveness. The park is easily accessible from Kailua-Kona, roughly a 45-minute drive. For those looking to immerse themselves in this historical experience, staying at the nearby Manago Hotel (82-6151 Mamalahoa Hwy, Captain Cook offers comfort and local charm, with room rates ranging from $75 to $150 per night.

On Maui, the village of Lahaina brings history to life. Once the capital of the Hawaiian Kingdom and a busy whaling port, today's Lahaina is a vibrant mix of old and new. Walking along Front Street, the historic facades blend with modern shops and eateries, all backdropped by the stunning Pacific Ocean. The Lahaina Inn (127 Lahainaluna Rd, Lahaina provides a cozy stay, nestled within walking distance of the famous Banyan Tree and the oceanfront. Rates typically range from $160 to $250. For dining in Lahaina, I recommend the Old Lahaina Luau (1251 Front St, Lahaina; for an authentic Hawaiian feast. Not only is it a culinary journey through the flavors of Hawaii, but also an evening filled with traditional music, dance, and storytelling, essential for understanding local customs and history. Each visit to these sites offers more than just a view of stone and sea; it's an educational journey steeped in the aloha spirit. Whether you're gazing upon the intricate petroglyphs at Puako Petroglyph Archaeological Preserve or wandering through the remains of an ancient village, you connect with the heartbeat of traditional Hawaii.

These journeys not only educate but also highlight the importance of preserving such treasures. By visiting responsibly and supporting local businesses, we help ensure that these glimpses into the past remain part of Hawaii's future. Always remember, when you explore these sacred sites, you walk on revered ground. Treat each visit with respect, tread lightly, and take only memories—a true traveler's homage to Hawaii's storied shores.

Sustainable Tourism: How to Visit Hawaii Responsibly

Traveling to Hawaii offers more than just a getaway; it presents an opportunity to engage with a unique ecosystem and vibrant culture in a way that can either nurture or deplete its precious resources. Understanding how to visit Hawaii responsibly isn't just recommended; it's essential.

As someone who deeply cherishes every visit to the islands, I've learned that sustainable tourism in Hawaii means more than just minimizing your carbon footprint. It involves immersing yourself into local traditions and supporting the economy in ways that respect and preserve its heritage and environment.

Opting for eco-friendly accommodations is a powerful start. Many Hawaiian hotels and resorts now prioritize sustainability through solar power, water conservation programs, and recycling initiatives. Places like the Hyatt Regency Maui

Resort and Spa, located at 200 Nohea Kai Drive, Lahaina have embraced solar power and water-saving fixtures that significantly reduce their environmental impact. Staying here, or at similar properties, supports businesses that are committed to Hawaii's ecological health.

Buying local is another key aspect of sustainable tourism. It supports the community economically and reduces the environmental impact associated with shipping goods to the islands. From farmers' markets in Hilo to the craft shops in Hanalei, spending your dollars on locally made products means investing in the community's sustainability.

Respect for culture is paramount. Participating in cultural workshops or visiting cultural heritage sites offers insights into the Hawaiian way of life and its history but do so with respect. Activities like small-group tours with local guides, such as those offered by Native Hawaiian Hospitality Association (NaHHA), encourage respectful engagement and education. These experiences not only enrich your visit but also ensure that tourism has a positive impact on the local cultural landscape.

Being mindful of your environmental impact while enjoying Hawaii's natural landscapes is crucial. Stick to marked trails when hiking, maintain a safe and respectful distance from wildlife, and never remove natural objects or artifacts from their sites. Organizations like the Hawaii Ecotourism Association offer certified sustainable tours that educate tourists on the islands' ecosystems while promoting conservation efforts.

Hawaii has been a leader in reducing plastic waste, being the first state to ban plastic bags. As a visitor, you can contribute by using reusable water bottles, shopping bags, and avoiding single-use plastics. Many local businesses offer alternatives, such as biodegradable containers and utensils, making it easier for tourists to make eco-friendly choices.

Each time I visit, I strive to leave Hawaii no less beautiful than when I arrived. Embracing sustainable tourism practices isn't just about enjoying this paradise; it's about preserving it for future generations to experience and cherish as deeply as we do today. By choosing to travel responsibly, we help ensure that the beauty of Hawaii remains vibrant and vivacious, rich in culture and natural splendor, just as it deserves to be.

CONCLUSION

As our journey through the Hawaiian Islands comes to a close, it's hard not to reflect on the unique experiences and profound beauty that encapsulate this magnificent destination. Hawaii offers more than just picturesque landscapes and warm, turquoise waters; it offers a deep dive into a vibrant culture steeped in tradition and a natural environment that is both enchanting and fragile.

Throughout our exploration, from the bustling streets of Honolulu to the tranquil shores of Lanai, each moment spent here reinforces the importance of traveling with intention and respect. Hawaii is not just a place to visit; it's a place to learn, to experience, and to give back to. As a traveler, it's crucial to recognize our role in preserving the very wonders that call us to these islands. Making sustainable travel choices has been a recurring theme in our discussions. Opting for eco-friendly accommodations, supporting local businesses, respecting cultural sites, and participating in conservation efforts are not just recommendations; they are responsibilities. Each decision we make leaves a footprint, and in Hawaii, where the balance of nature and culture is so vital, our footprints matter immensely. Visiting Hawaii gives us more than memories; it gives us lessons in the importance of cultural respect and environmental stewardship. The islands teach us about the fragility of our ecosystems and the strength of our cultural connections. They remind us that travel is not just about seeing new places but about understanding them and appreciating them in ways that go beyond the surface. As we pack our bags and prepare for our journeys home, the real voyage begins—not just in returning to our daily lives but in carrying forward the lessons learned here. How we talk about Hawaii, share our stories, and most importantly, how we apply our newfound insights into our actions at home, can foster a greater appreciation for cultural diversity and ecological preservation everywhere.

Made in the USA
Las Vegas, NV
17 April 2025